BLITZ KIDS

KENNETH BLACKBURN

Blackburn Books

First published by BBC Broadcast Books 4 Cotham Vale, Bristol BS6 6HR in
association with BBC Radio Bristol 1995

The BBC Radio series BLITZ KIDS was first broadcast in 1991, and then
rebroadcast in May 1995.

This revised version is designed for republication in 2020 as the content is soon
to become an International Feature Film.

ISBN 978-0-473-53183-6

A catalogue record for this book is available from the
National Library of New Zealand.

kenblackburn@xtra.co.nz

Cover illustration by John Blackburn

Text illustrations by John and Ken Blackburn.

The Author Ken Blackburn

KENNETH BLACKBURN

Born at the Bristol Royal Infirmary in April 1935, Ken was brought up in the St Paul's district of Bristol. Along with his older brother John, born in 1933. They were evacuees to the South West of England during the Second World War. After the war ended he and his family emigrated to New Zealand.

Ken has been a Free Lance Actor and Director now for over sixty years and has played a wide range of characters in Theatre, Radio, Film and Television. Notably among these have been.

Hank Blair in the series "White Fang" for Atlantis Films
Sir Bruce Warner in "Shortland Street"
The Boss in the series "Gliding On"

In the theatre he was awarded Best Actor as Vladimir in "Waiting for Godot." Best Actor as Davies in "The Caretaker" and appeared throughout Australia Canada and England in Stage performances. In 1974 he was honoured by the Polish Ministry of Culture with the "Amicus Poloniae" for fostering cultural relations between Poland and foreign countries. He was made a member of the New Zealand Order of Merit in 2006 and awarded the "Lifetime Achievement Award' in 2017.

Ken has a renowned expertise in accents and dialects which has often been called on for narration work and commercial voice overs. He narrated the BLITZ KIDS series for BBC radio Bristol

Today he lives in the North Island of New Zealand with his wife Carolyn, and they share their two storey colonial villa with their two dogs.

Gran and Aunty May

CHAPTER 1

I was born in the Bristol Royal Infirmary on the 2nd of April 1935 to Florence Elizabeth May Beachem and Albert Beachem. It was the time of the great depression and as they could not afford the required shilling for a birth certificate, they opted to pay one penny for a receipt which registered that a son had been born. Being the second child of this marriage. I was referred to as "Tuppence" for quite some time though eventually christened as Kenneth. My brother John had been born two years earlier.

I remember nothing at all of my father, though I note from the Somerset House copy of my birth certificate that he was labelled "Barman of Bristol." I've often wondered whether that was a prestigious position in the Bristol of 1935. Albert Frank Beachem made the decision to end his life in March 1937 and the close proximity to my birth has often given me cause for thought over the years. I asked the question "How did Dad die" and the least plausible answer my Mother came up with was that he was breaking up coal in the cellar and a piece flew up into his eye and killed him. Well, this satisfied me as a young child, but later the inconsistencies began to creep in, and there were times when she assured me that he had died of the flu. I think I was about thirty when the full truth was told.

My mother was a domestic worker at the time, also a frustrated nurse, schoolteacher and singer. She once sang at the Blackpool Tower and was a regular vocalist accompanying the recorded music at the local ice rink. But our family had a long heritage as working class Bristolians and how can I forget meeting my estranged Grandfather selling matches from a tray around his neck as he plied the streets My mother had no support for her ambitions from my Grandmother, herself, a professional domestic who had been "In Service" since she was nine years old. "Humph!" she'd say. "Getting ideas above your station my gurl." We lived in Monk Street in St Pauls district with my Aunty May (a spinster and older sister of Mum) Gran never wore anything other than Black as I recall and Aunty May smelt of tobacco. May had worked in the same room of a factory for over fifty years as a "Stripper" That was the title given to those that stripped tobacco leaves from their stems. She ended up in charge at the head of a table of girls doing this work at Wills Tobacco No.1.Factory in Bedminster. She died in the mid 1960s of lung cancer though never smoked a cigarette in her life.

I still see Gran, Aunty May and Monk Street very clearly in my mind. Standing at the end of the road where it meets Newfoundland Road there was a corner pub known as "Scapens" and here the entire street would gather in the evenings, and where we as children, sat outside on broad sills or on the pavement knowing that there was a chance of a lemonade or a bag of crisps being handed out of the window. I also recall the twist of blue paper containing salt being in these bags giving you the choice. There was a chance here too of making a few pennies as the evening wore on and it became easier to persuade customers to pay for a child's treble solo rendered through the open window. I was as heart broken as any adult when Scapens was devastated by bombs during a raid.

Although every house frontage was identical in Monk Street we regarded the next one along from Scapens as the posh one. It was occupied by a kindly old couple who kept it freshly painted, neatly curtained, and with a back garden that was neat, tidy and well gardened. This made it seem a better house than all the others. Or maybe it was because Gran and Aunty May lived next door.

It may never have been in the same state of pristine freshness, but a more vigorously scrubbed front doorstep would be hard to find. This doorstep entry and the plaster model of a "Whistling Boy" in the front window was Gran's statement to the world that people of "Quality" lived here.

There was an absence of men, or fathers in my early recollections even though war had yet to break out and my Gran somehow managed to take in Mum John and I to add to her trials on the demise of my father. I remember only my Uncle Sam visiting occasionally but there was never a man about the house to do the everyday maintenance work required and all the other houses seemed to have this. The frontage design of every house in the street was identical and owned by the City Council, taking weekly rent but never visiting for any reason other than collecting.

Monk Street

We had gas lamps both on the street and inside as there was no electricity. All cooking was done on a wood and coal stove and laundry work in a wood fire heated copper. Two bedrooms upstairs above the front room (Sacred Sanctuary) and the kitchen with a glasshouse extension to the outside lavatory and Anderson Shelter.

On the street the front door opened right onto the pavement across that scrubbed wooden entrance step. This continued in a straight line flush with a three foot wide pavement to the end of the street. Here you came up against a grey stone wall, the top of which my fingers could just reach to get a grip. Heaving yourself up, taking the leather off your toecaps in the process, you looked down into the River Frome. This was better known to local kids as the "DANNY" It had a great expanse of mud bank on either side with a channel of water about six feet across in the middle. I can still remember being in tears on this wall when a big lad of about 16 or so brought down a seagull with an air rifle and continued to fill it with pellets until it ceased fluttering.

Twice a day the Danny would flood with a tidal rush which I later learned to be called "The Roar".

If you walked along the Danny wall you could look into the back gardens of the houses right down Monk St. Most of them had an Anderson Shelter sunk into the ground made of corrugated iron sheets and a sacking entrance wherein you stood more chance of dying of pleurisy than being bombed. They had a roof usually covered with some gardening effort, maybe flowers or vegetables. At Gran's it was a special treat to sleep out in the shelter at night and pull carrots for a midnight feast, though at a later date it proved less fun to be confined to it for three days and four nights as Jerry flattened the city of Bristol.

When my mother took a basement flat at 79 Ashley Road opposite St Barnabas Church, John and I continued to attend Newfoundland Rd School until the time of evacuation. Mum went to work in the railyards at Temple Meads Station pushing rail wagons around and connecting them, alongside Italian prisoners of war. At night she was a Bar Room singer. Life was exciting and the intermittent raids bothered us less as time drew on in the war. John and I along with our street gang of Dennis Jay, Audrey, Snotty Fox (So called because of his constant runny nose) would meet regularly in the Anderson shelter at the back of Gran's house. We would attend all the local bombed sites, incendiary fires and other scenes of devastation following a raid. We all had our personal coveted collections of shrapnel, bullet cases, military badges, fins of incendiaries etc along with the customary marbles, conkers and cigarette cards of footballers. These were our units of currency to acquire the good things in life like sweets, chewing gum, comics or a "ride on yer bike" Road tar was in common use as a poor substitute for chewing gum and an envied owner would often lend it out for a few hours on a swap deal for comics,but never for keeps. My collection of shrapnel in a flat Capstan cigarette tin, boasted a special piece that everyone wanted to borrow. It was the jagged shard of a German shell that put my Uncle Sam out of the war. He was invalided out after being hit in the right elbow, and this prize piece of metal he had given to me for my collection. It was like having a prize conker and always swung the deal on any bartering that was needed. The only drawback to its ownership was the number of times my Uncle Sam needed to borrow it back, and regrettably it was on such an occasion that he borrowed my entire collection to impress the bar at "Scapens" and left it with the publican when he weaved his way home. It was that same night that Jerry chose to drop several sticks of incendiaries and high explosives around Newfoundland Rd. and Monk St. and I was certainly as heart broken as any adult when "Scapens" was devastated and my shrapnel went up..for the second time.

Woe betide if the driver saw you, that whip could reach right to the back.

CHAPTER 2

When Air Reich Marshall Goering started to become a little tetchy over the loss of so many German aircraft, and more particularly for the unstoppable efforts of the RAF in getting through to give Berlin such a pasting, he looked at a map of England and picked out the jewels in the crown for special treatment. These became known as the "Baedeker" raids, after a popular guide book of the time. Bristol was to be one of those jewels. Exeter was another, bombed in retaliation for the bombing of Essen but more of that later. Many well known features of Bristol were blitzed including "Lennards Corner" which was a huge department store. The Triangle Cinema. The Coliseum dance hall and skating rink where Mum sang and played the records. Bethesda Chapel on Brandons Hill. Merchants Hall which had stood since 1770. The Seamans Alms Houses (also 18th century) and very sadly Princes Theatre and the Dutch House. The docks at Hotwells and the Basin took a tremendous pounding and even Arnos Vale cemetery was bombed because it had appeared from the air to be rows of tents. All over the city there was a pox of craters, ruined football fields and shattered buildings with their acrid smell of incinerated timber. It always reminded me of kippers. When the vinegar factory went up in Newfoundland Rd there was a mouth watering smell in the air for days.

When I see a dolls house now with the roof off or a side removed I am reminded of those days and nights on the streets of Bristol. The humour within the tragedy was not lost on me at the age of seven and eight either, because the most vivid memories are those which revealed the more private aspect of people's lives when suddenly their homes would be "Open House" to the world. A free-standing wall with a staircase attached and the scorched wallpaper still decorated with pictures or family photographs hanging all askew. A top landing spring boarding into space. A fire still burning in the second floor grate of another house halfway up a wall and no way of putting more coal on unless you were thirty feet tall. Who was on the lavatory when the bomb hit? I wondered, because it was still flushing and the chain swung listlessly in the open air.

Looting at this time of crisis was a major problem throughout England and though as kids we were intent on souvenir collecting, It's not surprising that the Wardens, the Police and the Home Guard dealt with us severely if caught on a bombsite. Rightly so, though our intent was not of the measure of the major crime syndicates who often turned up in helmets and boiler suits, to rope off the area and remove truckloads of goods.

There was a factory which we knew as the Marble factory, though it actually produced bottles that had a marble in the crimped neck of them. When this was hit and all the officials had gone, it became something like King Solomon's Mines. We had a stakeout for excavation purposes each jealously guarded and fortified, and the process of recovering hundreds of clear marbles and Ginger beer stoppers went on for several weeks. Claims only changed hands for highly prized shrapnel, badges or bundles of Hotspur and Champion comics. There would be a couple of hours of this activity after school and then we would tear off home down the back streets to be home before dark and count out our booty. After a tiring day a more leisurely way of getting home was to sneak off the pavement up behind a horse drawn dray from Georges Brewery and hang off the back. Provided the driver didn't see you, you could travel quite a way with your elbows up on the dray and your shoes clipping the tops of the cobblestones. Woe betide if he saw you though. That whip could reach right to the back and most of them didn't mind using it. The leather and canvas bag of feed was always slung at the back until a pause in the days work. Then it would be slung over the horses ears at the other end of the vehicle.

The tasty, nut-like grain would often filter through the holes in our trouser pockets and my Gran would say ... "Ere, Wha's all these seeds doin' on my clean floor?" "I dunno Gran" we'd say. "Thee bist lyin'" she'd say. "No I baint Gran,honest".. "Well yers a clip round the ear, just in case".

How our Gran escaped the war is a mystery to me. She simply ignored it. She refused to leave the house and get into the Anderson shelter at the bottom of the garden when an air raid siren went. She just went about her planned routine of cooking, cleaning, boiling the washing, and ironing and generally "Doing for other people" while Bristol blazed all around her. "That bleed'n 'Itler" she'd mutter "I wish 'e'ad my feet". Then she'd lace on her black boots and head off into the crackling night to deliver ironing or pick up someones washing.

She might have made use of the other type of shelter had we been able to afford one. It was called a "Morrison Shelter" and it had all the appearance of an enormous rat trap. A large table top of steel plate that sat in the middle of the room and caged around with steel mesh with a small gate giving entry to one side. John and I experienced this rat trap when we were evacuated to Exeter. "Wha's thee think I am? Runnin' out the bleed'n house everytime the siren goes. Gord bleed'n 'Imey (Her version of Gor Blimey) I'm stop'n put. I got things to do" So the Air Raid Warden would often be banging on the door of 39 Monk Street shouting "Put that light out."as my Gran pressed on with her work in the greenish blue glow of the gas light filament.

It was, of course, essential to try and achieve a total blackout when Jerry was overhead, as the telltale lights of a populated area usually guaranteed the disgorgement of incendiaries and high explosives. None of this worried my Gran I might say. In fact. If she hadn't been so busy, she'd have gone over and dealt with Hitler on her own. Remember Old Mother Riley in those early films?? That was my Gran.

It was in April 1941 that Bristol and Coventry copped it really badly, and King George V1 came down to look around and talk to the people. It didn't mean much to me then, except that I remember laughing when Granny Hudd fell forward, losing her balance trying to curtsey to him. He talked to everyone, shook

15

hands and made everyone feel a lot happier. Not the case though when Churchill came down to Bristol, he was roundly booed everywhere he went. The king wore one of those posh camel hair coats and a peaked army hat (no crown) which was a surprise, and he stuttered a bit too. There was no doubt that he was everybody's hero.

"That bleed'n Hitler....I wish 'e 'ad my feet"

Air Raid Wardens were part of the Home Front Defence Corps, usually middle aged men in blue boiler suits and a steel helmet that said A.R.P. The ubiquitous gas mask was shoulder slung and they carried a stirrup pump for small fires. I had many opportunities to see them in action, controlling crowds, administering first aid and comforting the bereaved. I saw them too when their nerve gave out, as it did with one who joined us in a city shelter one night.

He crouched in a corner, trembling and his tears flowed freely. I'd never seen a man do that before. Some of these men saw more action than the younger ones at the front line, but they didn't wear the medals. They often worked all night during a raid and then continued without sleep through the day desperately digging out bodies or buried victims from their collapsed homes. They gave unsparingly of everything they could to keep up the morale at home.

Among the unsung heroes as far as I was personally concerned was Mary. Mary was a W.A.A.F. who worked at a Balloon Barrage Base situated in the woods very near to where John and I were later evacuated in Exeter. One of our many jobs was to scour the woods with a handcart and collect firewood, and it was on one of these occasions that we met Mary. She would have been about 18, I suppose, and she saw in us an opportunity to give that little bit extra for the war effort. We were delighted to be the benefactors in this case because it meant following Mary back to the base and waiting outside the window of a large Nissen hut until she passed out a plate of hot bacon, eggs and fried bread for each of us. This was a breakfast treat that we had never experienced before and it became a regular event during an otherwise miserable time in Exeter. I doubt that you would have found two more willing evacuees to go out in all weathers to collect firewood in all of England. Dear Mary! We could give nothing in return and to this day I don't know what she risked in doing this for us. She didn't wear any medals either, nor did we ever know who she really was.

The other heroes of my acquaintance were men who stood in the queues at the pictures. The line was always very long, but generally you didn't mind queues during the war, they were a way of life. People joined them to find out what they were for when they got to the front..soap, shoes, meat, fish or fags. But everyone knew when they were queueing for the pictures because a Commissionaire in braided uniform and cap walked up and down the line calling out seat prices and what was available. If you could afford the expensive ones you could leave the line and go in. "Three in the grand Circle at 2/6d Four Stalls at a shilling each and

I've got a pair in the gallery at threepence". There was a restriction on cinema attendance according to the certificate of the film. For instance, there was always two films showing and if they were both classified "U" or Universal Exhibition they were available to any age. If an "A" and a "U" were showing you could only attend in the company of an adult, whereas with two "A"s showing you had to be an adult to get in. In order to ensure that we didn't miss any of the latest popular films, we would seek out a likely prospect in the queue and boldly ask.."Hey Mister. Will you take us in we got our own money?" The fact that they usually did, wouldn't let you pay and also bought you a Walls ice cream at interval, places them among the heroes who didn't wear the medals.

Boys in the Anderson Shelter

CHAPTER 3.

"Three ha'porth of scrumps please!" I don't suppose one in ten million would know what you were talking about today, but you could hear it any night of the week in a crowded fish'nchip shop back in Bristol during the war. Admittedly, most people were there to buy fish and chips, but there'd always be a grubby kid with the arse out of his trousers and cardboard in his shoes trying to get served with "Three ha'porth of scrumps" Scrumps were the floating debris of batter bubbles and burnt chip that was scooped off the surface of the vat and dumped alongside. What a treat! Wrapped in the Daily mirror this was, and there was no charge for salt and vinegar. You could fold your cap around them and stuff them down your jersey for added insulation, then feed off them at leisure while creating an oil slick from your chest to your chin. I can taste 'em even now. Food and adequate heating were the priority then. John and I were living with Mum, Gran and Aunty May at Gran's house in Monk St. All the cooking was done on a large coal range in the parlour. It had lids, drawers, doors, pushed and pulled grates that dropped or lifted and vents that opened, all of which my Gran manipulated with the skill of an engine driver to cook up a meal. She also heated irons on it for clothes pressing and tongs for hair curling. It also dried out your boots when they were wet. The only food not prepared here was the Christmas Pudding. This was done in the copper out in the wash house. The stove was in fact the centre of our lives, and, as befitting such a monument it was cleaned inside and out then blackened with a product that today would have racial overtones. The mantelpiece above was fringed with a faded tasseled green velvet cloth and was crowned by small pictures and tinned treasures.These surrounded the "News" "I.T.M.A." Bebe Daniels and Ben Lyon and of course the "Andrews Sisters"..Yes!

The radio. At the apex of our lives it represented entertainment and information on the state of the war. At 9 o'clock each night nobody dared to speak for fear of missing some important item on the news. A drawstring to the side of the stove raised or lowered the ever present washing on a wooden stretcher and the hob was always occupied by wet socks, bare feet and wet boots. Keeping it fired brings back the two worst memories I have of my Gran. We had an old pram in the greenhouse. It was of the "Gracious Carriage" variety and it was big! Who knows, it was probably mine at an earlier age. It was brought out once a week for the collection of the coal. This particular exercise meant going with Gran on an excursion along the railway tracks. Trying to push a large and not well sprung vehicle over uneven stones, sleepers and railtracks, while picking up nubs of coal fallen from passing engine tenders was very hard work. However it was greatly outranked by the embarrassment attached to the other task that the pram was used for.. Around the corner from Monk St. and a short distance along Newfoundland Rd there was a vinegar factory. This factory transported large barrels on open drays drawn by enormous Clydesdale horses. My Gran was a badly failed horticulturalist, but she held an implicit belief in manure. So whenever a dray clopped its way down the cobbles of Monk St. or a similar wagon from Georges Brewery went past, Gran would thrust the hearth shovel at me and instruct me to follow with the pram, and, God willing! I would come home with a substantial steaming load for the garden, and, God Willing! Not meet any of my friends on the way. It was a mortifying experience.

Collecting manure for Gran's garden

Another memory of Gran involved the weekly trip that my brother and I had to make to collect the bread at Hotwells. I suppose it was a church charity house that provided it. I have a vivid memory of a high green door with black studs on it that had to be knocked upon. When it was opened by a large aproned woman, we presented Gran's coupon and from the long trestle table laden with crusty loaves we would be presented with two of them. We would then set off home but always with Gran's warning ringing in our ears. However, not all of the deliciously tempting warm bread arrived. We found ways of extracting a mouthful without changing the shape of the loaf too much and as Gran was often heard to remark. You don't set pigs to guard your pantry. On one occasion I was sent alone to get the bread as John was sick and while I was on the return from Hotwells, one of Jerry's daylight raids occurred. These were rare but effective and often came about as a bomber disgorged high explosives on return from major raids further north on Liverpool or Manchester. The siren wailed and I set off at pace taking all the shortcuts I knew whilst hugging the two loaves to my pounding chest. I ran hell for leather through back streets, lanes and bomb sites toward home. While clambering through one devastated bomb site, history repeated itself with a tremendous "BANG". Shrouded by a hail of bricks, pipes and dust, I lost consciousness. How long I lay there I don't now know but when I managed to get up I was aware of a pain in the stomach, a very bloody left foot and no shoe..but even more tragically. no bread! My Gran greeted me at the front door with the words "Ne'er mind thy foot. Where's the bleed'n bread?" Three bus loads of people were killed near College Green that day in 1942.

Black bread and margarine seemed to grace most tables, and although the name conjures up a sickening image, the bread referred to was actually grey due to the poor quality of the flour at the time. The margarine was another story altogether. It certainly didn't have the flavour of today's butter substitute and even now my stomach revolts at the memory of this white paste that tasted like rubber. My revulsion for it was recognized at home and it was only while evacuated that the nightmare grew as I was compelled to force it down. Jam sandwiches or bread and dripping were school lunches for us. School dinners were available but these cost fourpence a week and there were a lot more of us that couldn't afford that than could. I do remember Miss Fisk our teacher would give you a cup of tea at lunchtime if you brought your own cup. Newfoundland Rd School was a ten minute walk from Monk St. That was if you went straight there and didn't divert over bomb sites looking for shrapnel or souvenirs, but it was a two minute run home where you divested yourself of coat, cap and gas mask then got back into the street where the real world was. Sometimes we all met in the Anderson shelter for a swap session or to discuss the news. I don't mean grown up war news either, that was boring. The war was happening over our heads and was something we had come to accept. No, we had cigarette cards, comics, badges and school news that we needed to deal with. There was a major issue at stake called "EVACUATION" and we needed to plan for that. The boys held counsel and Audrey did "handstands" When major issues and swaps were resolved we would gather in Monk St. It was cobbled and had a gutter running down the centre of it and here we ran our regattas and races with matchbox boats and Woodbine packets. There we would be until the light was too dim to sail or we were called in for tea and then bed. Food was set on a kitchen table that Gran scrubbed every day. "You bleed'n tykes'll be the death of me one day" she'd say "C'mon our Flar"(This was my Mother whose name was Flo) "Wher's our Mary Ann then?" and when Aunty May joined us we would settle at the table for the evening meal. Aunty May was the most stable factor in the family as she had been at work from the age of 15 at Will's Cigarette factory in Bedminster. She was warm and cheery with a lap to match and always arrived home with the Daily Mirror and sweets. It seems she almost got married once. She was certainly engaged. The front room of 39 Monk St. was like a sanctuary, though not a comforting one. Everything in it seemed to be "entombed" and I looked in most often through the front window from the street. Gran would never allow us to enter the room. If the light was right you could just see in between the gap in the lace curtain and the "Whistling Boy" statue that guarded its secrets. It was many years later that Aunty May took me into the room and here one by one she fondled and explained the precious engagement presents that were housed in a glass fronted bureau. There was even the earliest type of electric iron still in its box. Crystal pieces and decorated cups and saucers all on display but none were ever used. They represented a memorial to a failed relationship and she died a spinster. Plagued throughout her working life by a persistent rash on her feet that was tobacco induced, she and Gran shared a soothing foot bath in the evening.

Aunty May washing her feet

CHAPTER 4.

The strain on nerves from persistent bombing, brought about an offer of voluntary evacuation from many big cities and thus began a new chapter in the social fabric of England. I can recall the trauma of that separation at Temple Meads Station. It was in early May 1942 and 18,500 elementary school children between the ages of 5 and 15 assembled there over a three day period to be sent off to other parts of the West of England. To so called "Safe Ares" Old decommissioned railway carriages were put back into service and most had no toilets. The lines were clogged to such an extent that many short journeys took an entire day to reach their destination. Is it any wonder that the state of many youngsters gave their foster homes cause for regret at having volunteered. As it happened the volume of evacuees was so great that adult families known to have rooms in their houses were compelled to open their doors and so become "reluctant foster homes". The consequences of this can never now be measured. A warning flag to the authorities might have been signalled by the fact that within 3 months.. 9,500 of those Bristol children had returned home by many and various ways.

I stood on the main platform with my brother John waiting to board a train, destination vaguely known as "The Beach" We had one bag between us, a luggage label pinned to our coats declaring name and a number. We had been given a postcard to send home in a week's time saying where we were. The string slung gas mask in a cardboard box was over the shoulder. From end to end the platform was choked with emotional partings and many mothers were contained behind large iron gates. Not even a handful of licorice allsorts from the A.R.P. man could alleviate the misery. It transpired that we were bound for Weston Super Mare on the coast, something of a holiday town with a pier. It had a fun reputation for the beach, amusements like Punch and Judy and also Donkey rides on the golden sands. When we arrived in 1942 the tide was out and an expanse of derelict beach was covered in barbed wire."Prohibited" signs were everywhere and even paddling was strictly out of bounds. No amusements on the closed pier and no donkeys. The lady, Mrs Sanford, met us on the station in the evening gloom. She lived in a semi-detached two storey house in Southville Rd along with her husband. She was welcoming and kindly as she took us in and here we met Mr Sanford and three other evacuees who were already there.

Ready for the Evacuation

She was what we might call an "amply proportioned" woman, while Mr Sanford was half her height and a third her weight. He was further diminished by the loss of his right forearm in the first world war. The stump, covered by a sock and an elastic band was a forbidding sight to a seven year old boy, and as time later proved, a fearsome weapon in the many episodes wherein he swung in a foreshortened attempt to hit you with it. Perhaps he'd always been right handed and never came to terms with the disability in times of stress. Certainly a slap with the left hand would have been more effective in the short term and less damaging to one's dreams in the long term. They kept a Budgie in a cage for which they both reserved a seldom heard tone of affection. It soon became apparent that this blue feathered tweeter was the sole recipient of affection in the Sanford household. They had a daughter in the W.A.A.F.s who worked nearby and a son in his twenties that came and went often so there was considerable strain on the bedroom accommodation. It soon became apparent that the five evacuees would be sharing a double bed in the upstairs front room. As the youngest and smallest I occupied the lateral position at the foot of the bed and, of course, endured the company of the four pairs of feet that lay lengthways in the conventional manner. When Mrs Sanford came to lock the door (don't know why!) she would wave about a sprig of burning lavender to counteract the juvenile flatulence. I was rather more stunned by the feet, I must say. The eldest evacuee at 15 had the same Christian name as me. Kenneth, and I suppose his age automatically gave him priority rights. Anyway, I was renamed "Jimmy" by the Sanfords and effectively lost my identity for almost nine months.

I suppose the benefits of throwing open one of your bedrooms to five strange children during the war were few, though I later learned that those who were kind enough or compelled to also received variable payments from the government. At the very least 10 shillings a head per week or 12/6d if they were a bedwetter. The percentage of bedwetters rose very sharply when this was known. While not denying that many children became "Enuretic" through separation anxiety.

Mr and Mrs Sanford

Ration books were your lifeline and every man, woman and child had one. The pages of coupons therein, or points, as they were called, governed your allowance of meat, eggs, fruit and sweets. You were allowed four rashers of bacon a month, four eggs, two oranges, four ounces of sweets, and so on. Anything desirable that you saw in shops seemed to have the verbal attachment. "You can't have that. You haven't got enough points, my love." So, because of their obvious value to everyone, the ration books of all were spirited away to a bureau drawer in the main bedroom downstairs for safekeeping and judicious administration. In fact, the rare illuminated manuscripts of a monastic order could not have benefitted more from this degree of safekeeping as we never set eyes on them, or their entitlements again during our time at Southville Rd. They became, however, the key to my memory bank on this particular evacuation episode, because when we all five resolved to run away and get home again, we knew we couldn't leave without our ration books. Months of misery ensued as, along with the other evacuees, 15 year old Ken, Dennis and Peter, we struggled to survive. The meagre rations we ate and the random hidings we received for little reason along with the lack of acceptance by kids at the local school where we were known as "The Vacs" Our presence did seem to be detrimental to a prior smooth running of life in Weston. All these events along with the unpalatable food served to us at a separate table from the well laden one used by the Sanfords, simply hardened our resolve. On the appointed night that we chose to abscond and being the youngest and the smallest, I was the one to negotiate the trail to the bureau in the Sanford's bedroom. I had to exit the bedroom and make my way by the upper landing window (the stairs were locked off) across the greenhouse roof of glass, down a pipe and into the back garden. From here I was to enter through the back door,always unlocked because the lavatory was outside. Not for our use mind you, because we had a chamber pot in the bedroom. The task was to enter the main bedroom without waking them and remove the five ration books from the bureau. I then had to ascend the stairs and release the others so that we could exit the house by the front door. As it happened, I came away with seven ration books, but that's another story. Meanwhile the older Ken, my brother John along with Peter and Dennis dressed in their clothes and gathered their few possessions. We crept our way to freedom, although without much thought except perhaps defiance I went back in briefly and released the budgie from its cage. I had gathered Mr Sanford's trouser belt also and we jubilantly made our way to the railway station at 4am, pausing briefly to tear up the unwanted ration books and posting the belt into a pillar box marked Royal Mail. We were buoyed by the knowledge that soon we'd be home again with Mum. To get onto the platform at Weston it was necessary to cross a covered in overhead bridge. It was when we were mid way across this bridge that hearts leapt into mouths as we saw a flashing torch searching the darkness at the other end. As a group we quickly contrived to be a pile of luggage by sitting on the baggage and throwing Ken's big raincoat over us desperately hoping that he would pass us by.

The policeman on Weston Super Mare station overhead bridge

Unfortunately, the deception failed to work on this astute Weston copper on his night beat. We told him that we had run away and had to get a train back to Bristol. Big Ken said he had to get to London and Dennis wanted Liverpool. He listened sympathetically and then assured us that we would be allowed to run away tomorrow but for now we had to return to Southville Rd. I for one believed him implicitly.. He was a policeman. This proved to be, something of a turning point in my future belief in the word of authority.

So, we were turned in to a fuming Mr and Mrs Sanford taking it in turns for the thrashing that was inevitable. I often consoled myself that it was Jimmy and not me who took these hidings. There were many lectures over the next few weeks about the value of ration books and I was up for considerable blame for the whole affair when Big Ken blurted out that it was me who released the budgie. However I did enjoy a sense of individual heroism because my punishment entailed eating on my own in the scullery and the others would pinch extra food from the table to give me extra treats out of compassion. I'm sure those days sowed in me the seeds of truculence and cynicism however, and seeing the humour in most of these situations did not endear me to the Sanfords. Fancy putting me at a table on my own, with minimal servings of food, and an empty budgie cage. It made me laugh in spite of myself. Only another clout with the stump brought forth the tears. I think I learned not to cry because I knew it was expected and I was reluctant to give them that satisfaction. I also convinced myself that this wasn't happening to me, I was an impartial observer. "Where's that Jimmy?" "Jimmy, you come here and clean this up"

"You can all go, but Jimmy's stopping home". So you see, it wasn't me. It was that little bugger Jimmy. When John and I planned our escape from Weston we were somewhat helped by the stir caused when Peter's mother arrived to take him home the performance orchestrated for her visit was not lost on us. We all sat in the front room. A room we had never been in before. All five evacuees were seated on the couch. There was tea in matching cups and saucers and a big plate of sliced seed cake. Mrs Sanford had found a different voice from somewhere and used it to glide Peter's mother into an armchair. Throughout their tea party talk wherein Peter was given a status that he had never enjoyed before, many watery smiles were aimed at the rest of us by Mrs Sanford. Her every comment was backed up by a devoted husband who stood beside her seated figure, which had the amusing effect of giving them the same height. "Never, never had there been five more happy and contented children than these very fortunate evacuees. With the help of a good husband, who, by the way, was more than willing to serve again, but, see for yourself. The money can't come anywhere near what it costs to feed them. But you do what you can to support the war effort. They are absolutely devoted to us, and..I don't know what we shall do when it's all over and we have to hand them back." It was at about this point in the "charade" that Dennis farted. This was not so much a comment as a punctuation that sent us all into paroxysms of laughter. It was also a timely moment for Mrs Sanford to desperately cover by suggesting. "More tea Mrs er..um" Her departure along with Mr Sanford who helped her carry the teapot,saw Peter fly across the room into his mother's arms. I think it was only then that we realized that she was one of us. Peter's small case had been packed and there was an apple on top with his ration book. When the teapot returned and the cake was eaten, an astonishing piece of information was released. It seems that every ration book had to be registered with the local shops. Peter's mother had no use for the old one and she flourished a new ration book in Peter's name. This revelation meant simply that we had no need to feel anchored in Weston Super mare. We could just walk! Just simply walk, at any time. So, a couple of days later, we did. John and I went to school as usual, and, at the end of the day we set out on the road to Bristol instead of going home to "Stalag" Southville. This was the beginning of a realization that we were not alone in our endeavours to get home as we came across others flitting their way across the west of England, but more of this later. It took ages to get out of town and onto country roads, but when we did it must have been obvious to road users that we were on a greater mission than just going home for tea. Who helped us along the way I can't recall as I think I slept most of the way. I would like to know what was said by big Ken and Dennis in order to cover our escape as long as possible. I don't remember their other names and we never saw them again. I was just so happy to arrive back in Bristol as Ken and leave Jimmy in Weston.

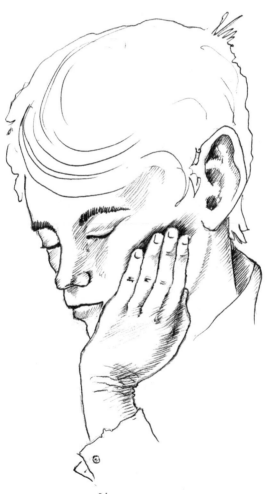

I learnt not to cry

CHAPTER 5.

"Piss freely for four hours". Well, that's what it said in the directions in the packet. Was it possible? The small brown envelopes were to be found everywhere in Bristol during the months of 1943. They were a free supply to American Servicemen and must have been dropped by plane like propaganda leaflets. We collected them from everywhere. They could be found in prolific amounts in most shop doorways, the docks and pub pavements and in bulk from the G.I. Dumps. The small brown envelope contained a balloon that was rolled up and a white paper with directions on it, the most memorable of these being "Following intercourse, piss freely for four hours", I later realised that this meant "as often as you can". The yanks had been around for some time and I recall how much smarter they looked in their top quality gabardine uniforms, alongside our own British Tommies in often ill matching blanket type khaki. Looking back I suppose injured pride played some part in the many scuffles that broke out. Mind you, the biggest riot that we witnessed was between the Yanks themselves as they came to severe blows with their own Black Regiment that was segregated and stationed in Bristol. When I learned later that the Americans were in England for two years before going to the Front, I'm amazed that the attrition rate wasn't higher than at Guadalcanal. They had it all, it seemed, smart uniforms that attracted the girls, money to spend, gifts galore and interminable leave. Military badges, shrapnel and cigarette cards were the currency among Bristol kids and the arrival of the Yanks added French letters, comics and Chiclets as units of exchange. A goodly supply of any of these could supply you with a life on easy street, though if you had a sister, things might have been a thousand fold better. At least, that was my eight year old assumption, because it was the question most often asked me by the Yanks.

The "Mauretania" was a pub in Park Street that had been built using the salvaged material from a sunken ship of the same name. Its windows were the old portholes, many of which found our noses pressed against them at night, listening to the strains of songs such as "I'll see you again" or "Somewhere in France with you". My mum was a singer there and would entertain nightly when she had finished pushing heavy wagons up and down the Goods yard at Temple Meads Station during the day. Those officers whose uniforms were slung carelessly or hurriedly about our sparse apartment in Ashley Road were probably unaware, until they raised an arm in salute, that their tunic had lost a button, a badge or a decoration of some kind. I had a good collection as the average American tunic seemed to be heavily endowed with ribbons and medals. The Yanks traded in silk stockings, candy bars cigarettes and comics of all kinds which they seemed to procure very cheaply at a place they called the PX. But we soon came to know that every G.I. Camp had its own freely dispensing cornucopia of these things which they called the "Garbage" The average G.I. garbage dump was the most amazing supermarket of tinned and packet goods, footwear, socks, containers of cereals, chiclets, comics and comestibles of all kinds..camp beds and steel lockers, cartons of cigarettes and boxed cigars etc the list is endless. Who was it that coined the phrase "Over supplied, Oversexed, and Over here" as the three main criticisms of the American Forces? There seemed to be much truth in the first part anyway. Since the loss of my shrapnel collection with the bombing of "Scapens" pub, I'd concentrated on badges and comics mostly, as these were easily tradeable with other kids. However, the advent of the French letter packets. With instructions, and the ever ready need for cigarettes, opened up a whole new market for me among adults. I set out to accumulate a stock of both.

Swapping, bartering, wheeling and dealing saw me get through such prizes as a "King Conker" a bag of blood orange marbles, or "Aggies" as we called them. A piece of barrage balloon that was burnt round the edges, bundles of Champion comics and even a piece of metal from a downed Messerschmidt.

Gottnee gum chum?

All had passed through the ever outstretched hands of "Our gang" in exchange for stock that we all sought.

It was about this time that my mother married again. Charlie Waters was his name and I remember him as a thin man in a grey suit. The only other memory I have was the clip over the ear as he confiscated my collection of 500 cigarettes in a large flat Craven A tin and the Bisto box filled with carefully stacked French letters "plus instructions" We never saw much of Charlie Waters because it happened at a time when John and I were between billets and very soon after his arrival we were evacuated to a place called

Devizes. I think it may have been friends or relatives of Charlie Waters that we were sent to. It was certainly arranged quickly and was no doubt convenient to have us in a bedroom thirty or so miles away than just next door. In retrospect, the decision to place this little town in Wiltshire on the list of "safe" areas must have come to the war office directly from Herman Goering, because it was the site of the biggest army base in the U.K. at the time. Small wonder then, that we were back at Ashley Rd within a month having been bombed out twice. On the latter occasion we woke to find that we were the only house left standing in the street. John and I often referred in later life to this second foster home in Devizes. Don't remember the lady's name but she had two teenage daughters who were sadists. We never had so many baths in all our lives, certainly we had no more aversion to soap and water than any other kids of our age, but being dumped in the galvanized tin bath every night seemed a bit excessive. Worse than that though, was the fact that we were scrubbed. These two daughters from hell took to us with stiff scrubbing brushes that were normally used on the floors. Every night this ritual took place in spite of the tears and the pleading. Thank God! Relief finally arrived when several high explosives wiped out the street and left this house of horrors leaning over the street at a 45 degree angle. It made it unstable and so it was condemned. A shame in a way because that was a door I'd like to have knocked on when I returned there at the age of 21.

Being scrubbed at bath time by a teenage sadist

CHAPTER 6.

As a child I associated Cheddar with cheese and not the Gorge which is to be found some miles south of Bristol, and John and I were to be evacuated to a new foster home near Cheddar Gorge. As we had been bombed out of our last billet in the (so called) safe area of Devizes, we were returned home, for which we were very grateful to the German High Command. We didn't find Mum very pleased though, for our succession of unsatisfactory billets was beginning to brand us with a bad reputation. The billeting authorities in Bristol were given to much tongue clicking and heavy sighs when the Beachem boys were mentioned. There was some whispered talk that we might end up being sent to Kingswood Reform School. I knew about this place in Bristol because Audrey told us that her brother was sent there for stealing. Anyway, for now it was Cheddar! The bus journey was to take about three hours laden with mothers and children. We were given emergency rations- a tin of corned beef, a tin of condensed milk and a slab of milk chocolate each. These were in our bag for about ten minutes before we decided to declare an emergency and open the chocolate. All the kids were smeared with it before long. We stopped at small villages here and there and some would get off, until finally the bus was left with just six evacuees going to Cheddar. It was dark when we arrived and an A.R.P. warden ushered us into a school or church hall where we were given more sweets and a chance to use the lavatory. Some other evacuees were already there and had come in from other cities. For some unknown reason we had to bed down for the night in this hall, and while stretched out on straw palliases with our heads on gas mask cases, the warden filled us in with some local history. We were somewhere in the Mendip Hills and he told us of nearby cave called "Wookey Hole"..a scary name, I thought. He described how the caves were formed and that they had names like "Hell's Passage" "Witches Parlour" and "Witches Hall and Kitchen" these were named after a witch who lived there in the Middle Ages. He said that she ate the local children. I don't know about John but I certainly didn't sleep that first night. Breakfast was brought in by the W.V.S and we had porridge with real cream, toast with jam and steaming tin mugs of sweet tea. All through that day people were coming and going as evacuees were taken to new billets. Once or twice John and I were called forward and we were looked up and down-we felt like we were in a jumble sale. What was happening was that the local villagers who were taking evacuees came and looked you over and if they liked you they signed for you and you went. I think they were well paid mind you, not a lot to be said for patriotism. Ten shillings a week plus a ration book and in our experience so far, an extra pair of hands for housework plus half a crown more if you were a bedwetter, which John was. The average wage at this time was only about three pounds. The onset of a second night in this hall saw the arrival of more evacuees and it began to look less and less likely that we would be chosen. There was also an impending repeat of the previous night's horror stories for the new arrivals to be considered. John pulled out the tail of his vest to polish his badly cracked glasses and said to me. "Grab yer things,we're goin' home" We dropped our bag out of the window behind us then asked if we could go to the lavatory. The A.R.P. man said. "You can't go together. The littlun can go first and when he comes back you can go" I was thunderstruck because we'd intended to go past the lavatory and out of the next door which exited the hall onto a graveled road. John hissed "You go on, I'll be out in a minute"

I was sweating as I stepped out into the cold night and I didn't know which way to go. I thought I'd better go around the back and pick up our bag. The grass was long and wet and it was very dark because of blackout precautions. I tried to remember the shape of the hall inside and work my way around to the window. As I groped my way nearer to where it should have been there was a muffled thump up ahead. I froze rigid in the long wet grass till John came up to me out of the gloom."I jumped out of the window" he said, "and you gotta help find me glasses, they came off" He dragged me back to the window and recovered the corned beef and condensed milk which he stuffed down the front of my overcoat.He then found his glasses by treading on them, which didn't help much and dragged me to the side of the road."Hurry up" he said." Or they'll catch us.. Why're you walkin' like that ? Oh God No! You've gone and done it in yer trousers 'avent you".

I doubt that John's eyes benefitted much from his glasses. He looked sideways to compensate for the cracks in his lenses

CHAPTER 7.

With no knowledge of geography and an even vaguer sense of how far we were from home, we set out along the tree lined road that led somewhere away from the church or school hall we had left in the Mendip Hills. John took the tins of corned beef and condensed milk to his own pockets once he'd seen that I had difficulty walking. He was nine and I was seven, and we were determined to get back home once again following this third attempt by the authorities to evacuate us from home and Mother. We must have spent an hour in darkness putting distance between us and the hall. It was cold and it was occasionally raining. I was in considerable distress and in need of water to clean myself up. We moved off the road and into farmland hoping to find a trough or a haystack, but there seemed to be nothing but moors and rocky outcrops as far as we could see. I took to carrying my trousers and had my overcoat safety-pinned between my knees for warmth. A stone crib built to give animals shelter in severe weather gave us our first protection and I dipped my trousers in the rough trough that it contained. We hammered at the corned beef tin with stones in an effort to get at the meat inside, but all to no avail. When you find yourself both hungry and tired, one desire always predominates over the other and we fell into a deep sleep wrapped together against the cold winds of the moor. By the time we woke the warm sun was up and had almost baked us dry, and thankfully I was able to wear my trousers again. John walked a bit higher up for a look and when he returned, he drew in the dirt with a stick. "We're up here and down below us there is the road. There's a village off to the right and a big town further on." He paused to sniff up and wipe his runny nose on his sleeve." Over t'other side of this hill though, there's a farmhouse with a big chicken run!"

His eyes tilted to mine and we said, quietly together "EGGS"

No further thought of journeying home could be entertained until we had something to eat. At this time we were still wearing our transit luggage labels with names and numbers. We tore these off and buried them under a small pile of stones, along with the condensed milk and the corned beef. Hidden by a copse of trees we came right up to the wire of the chicken run and watched for a while for any sign of human activity. There seemed to be no one about. The hens made a lot of noise when we lifted the latch of the gate and entered the run. Moving very quickly we put about eight eggs in John's rolled up jersey front and turned to make a rapid exit. Then she spoke. "You must be real hungry to be doin' that then," and her rosey face poked out from the inner hen house. "Where'd you two come from?" John and I couldn't speak for a minute, we never dreamed there'd be anyone inside there. She was the wife of the farmer and she turned out to be a wonderfully warm and caring lady, not the least bit cross with us as we were expecting her to be. There was no telling off, and no hiding. She took us into the house and gave us a full breakfast of bacon and eggs. In between mouthfuls we told her we had been evacuated from Bristol to a town up the road, but because the lady got sick we were allowed to go home."What town was that then?" she asked. John spluttered bits of egg, coughed and thought for a bit, then scratching his head he turned to me saying "What was it called Ken? D'you remember?" My eyes were on my plate as I shook my head vigorously. She seemed to chuckle a lot at everything we said as she made a warm bath for us.

As we sat facing each other and soaping up, her husband came in and she repeated our story to him. He sucked thoughtfully on a pipe and grunted and nodded. In his thick Somerset accent he said "Well boys, oim pleased you niver run off wi'moi aigs. When you'm droi Oi'll tek you in the village n' see the Vicar, he'll know what t'do". The farm lady gave us sixpence each and helped us up onto the back of the open draycart. As we made our way toward the village with our feet dangling over the back edge, John enquired "Where you taking us then Mister?" "The village" he said." Where's that?"asked John. He removed his pipe to use as a pointer."Down ther' Tha's Wookey. And way over yonder, tha's Wales" Our eyes brightened and there was a quick flash of something shared between us, because we both know that Wales was quite close to Bristol, so we must be headed in the right direction. Few road signs were to be seen as the threat of German invasion saw them all removed to confuse the enemy. Local knowledge was the best compass to any destination. We thought we were heading for home, but "A little knowledge is a dangerous thing". None the less, we had no wish to waste time with the local Vicar and perhaps end up back in the Church hall. Our Somerset farmer continued to talk and point with his pipe until he was out of earshot and we were watching from behind a hawthorn hedge till he rounded the next bend. We then headed off very fast through a field of turnips.

On the Mendips we hid in stone cribs or haystacks and worked our way towards Bristol

CHAPTER 8.

John and I scuttled across the field of turnips and into a ditch on the far side. In all probability the Somerset farmer was still talking and pointing out landmarks with his pipe, not knowing that we had dropped off the back of his cart some five minutes before. We had no wish to be taken to the local vicar for interrogation and possible return to the authorities. The farmer had pointed out Wales to us on the skyline and we knew that Bristol was nearby. Our Aunty May often talked about having her holidays over in Wales. We pressed on over more fields of turnips or beet and, keeping to the low level of the ditches whenever we saw the Land Army girls working, we pressed on all the time towards Bristol and Wales. Late in the afternoon the thunder of an approaching storm and a blackening sky added to our certainty that we wouldn't be in Bristol that night, but we kept going with the blind instinct that drives all sensible reasoning from your mind. Sloshing our way along the ditches we came across a boy with his little sister in hand, she was crying and he was angry with her. He said they had left their billet in Bideford a few days ago and were also heading for Bristol. We all knew that four couldn't travel as easily as two so we pressed on leaving him with his wailing sister. When it became almost too dark to see we came upon a road that led us toward a cliff face, and a stone pillar bore a metal plate announcing that this was the entrance to "WOOKEY HOLE". Although torrential rain had begun, we both found renewed energy and a carefree disregard for the discomfort of wet clothes in our resolve to stay on the road and bypass the dry caves. Our A.R.P. man had told us all we needed to know of "Hells Passage" and the "Witches Kitchen". The remembered story of Witches that ate children put wings on our heels. We spent the rest of the night in a damp haystack fitfully dozing, coughing and waiting for the daylight to reappear. In the morning we got a lot further on our way when a Land Army girl spotted us and gave us a ride on her tractor. She shared her sandwiches and cake with us too, and because she had a trailer full of turnips and apples, we soon became very full and so did our pockets. When she had to turn off the road John and I decided that this was the best way to travel and that we would wait for another vehicle to come along. This way we could be home by teatime. We didn't have long to wait! As the little black car eased to a stop beside us, my heart skipped a beat or two because the driver wore the reversed collar of a clergyman. It must be the Vicar that the farmer was taking us to. Rather reluctantly we climbed aboard the little Austin 7.. He asked our names and where we were going. "Are you the Vicar?" asked John. "No I'm not" he said, laughing. "I was at one time, but now I am the Dean of Wells Cathedral" We weren't sure what that meant but decided he was OK because he gave us a bar of Frys Cream Chocolate. We'd never been in a car before and we wondered why he had a swastika on the gearstick (Was he a spy??) He patiently dealt with all our questions before asking again where we were headed for. "We're going home to Bristol" I said. "Oh, You're a long way from there boys, and you're heading in the wrong direction" "No" said John, "Bristol's near Wales and Wales is up ahead". "Oh dear no!" said the Dean "I'm afraid you've been misinformed, up ahead is WELLS not WALES I know because I've lived there for many years." Our hearts hit the pits of our stomachs at this news and we sank into a disappointed silence until the Dean drove through some large gates and up to his house. We thought he must be pretty rich to live in a house this big and he had servants as well as a cook.

We feasted on rice pudding and bread and jam in the kitchen while the Dean busied himself elsewhere in the house. The cook was a bit like our Gran, and when we'd eaten she showed us the Parlour and the Library – I'd never seen so many books. When the Dean reappeared he asked if we would like to meet some other Bristol boys. "Yeah All right" we said, not knowing how he was going to manage that.. he then took us in his car to a house a few streets away and John and I couldn't believe our eyes. Here in the town of Wells were two of our friends from Newfoundland Road School. Tony, and Gordon Bates. They had been evacuated here about a month ago and were living with an elderly couple who ran a drapery shop in the main road. What a time we had that night, John and I in one bed and Tony and Gordon in the other talking till late about home and the bombing, our escape from Weston Super Mare and our more recent experience in the Mendip Hills and Wookey Hole. They were pretty homesick too but they were comfortable and well looked after. They even liked the school they were at in Wells. They used to live in Byron St. quite close to our old school. We didn't play much together because we were in different classes, but we knew them well. Before going to sleep we told them of our resolve to get back home come what may. We knew the Dean had prevailed on the old couple to take us in and see how we turned out, but we had no intention of staying longer than that one night. When the next day dawned we put our plan into operation.

The Dean of Wells. "Would you like to meet some other Bristol boys?"

CHAPTER 9.

It had been a big surprise for John and I to find two other evacuees from our school living with an elderly couple in Wells. After spending a warm night there and fortified with breakfast we set off with Tony and Gordon for the local school. We had no intention of completing the journey, mind you, but we had to agree because the Dean had made all the arrangements. However we weren't completely without honour as we decided to leave the sixpence each that we had on the bedroom sideboard. Tony had shown us his school atlas which provided us with a better idea of which way to go in our intention to get to Bristol. Up till now we had been travelling blind since Cheddar and the Dean had brought us well inland to Wells when we thought we were heading for Wales. Signs continued to be sparse or misleading because of the threat of German invasion. Wells was not a large town and we soon found ourselves in open country again. The boys had given us their school lunches as they said they could easily get more.We now had to face the Mendip Hills again and some open cast coal fields but the road led easily to Chewton Mendip and after that it would only be about another twelve miles to Bristol. We climbed and puffed for most of that morning and carried our coats for a good part of it as it was very warm. We were no longer encumbered with a bag of clothes or our gas masks as these had been left behind some time ago when we ran away from the church hall. We ate our sandwiches on a bluff overlooking the road. We knew we had to keep the main road in sight at all times but our lesson had been learnt to avoid being seen or assisted by well meaning people. As a result we took many diversions around thick brambles and streams, which resulted in scratched bleeding legs and wet shoes and socks. When we stopped for a rest in the afternoon on a higher piece of ground, we could see a lot of activity up ahead. It was the coal mine workers coming and going about their work, so we had no choice but to take to the road again. We decided to try and sleep then and see how far we could get by walking the road in the darker hours of night. It wasn't really possible to sleep in the bright glare of the afternoon but the rest eased our tiredness and as the sun left it became noticeably colder. So we set off. The fog came down and it was damp and eerie. We held hands and took to singing as we padded along the side of the road. We'd learnt a lot of songs from listening to Mum at home and when we joined her at the Ice Rink. People said she looked and sang like Dorothy McGuire the film star. It passed the time and gave us a rhythm for walking, it also helped to give us the feeling that we were not alone out there. It was very late and I suppose we were unguarded by tiredness when a vehicle came up from behind and picked us up in the headlights. We were in a cutting at the time and there was just no escape. There we stood like two blinded hedgehogs caught in a narrow band of light. "Hey kids, how ya doin'? kinda late getting' home from school huh?" It was an American Army jeep preceding a convoy of trucks. A soldier in a peaked cap came toward us with a cheery grin, and following a short version of our story he hoisted us onto the back of one of the trucks with a load of friendly chattering yanks. They plied us with chewing gum, chocolate and a multitude of questions. They were based somewhere between Chewton Mendip and Bristol and had been on night manoeuvres. So we roared on in warm comfort through the dark toward home and all the time denying that we were German spies or Parachutists. When we pulled up inside the camp the officer detailed one soldier to see that we got supper and a bed and two grateful evacuees slept till late next morning knowing that Chewton Mendip was well behind us. We had also been told that a supply truck would be taking us as far as Knowle on the outskirts of Bristol. We knew our way from there day or night. We were piled up with comics, Hershey bars and Chiclets when we finally left on the supply truck and the next few miles saw us make numerous stops where we helped the G.I. Corporal load and unload goods. As it had been a late departure the best part of the day had long gone and it was twilight over Bristol when we jumped down onto the Main Rd in the suburb of Knowle. John and I smiled when we looked up at the sign. It was WELLS Rd. We quickly made our way through many bombed streets toward Temple Meads but we didn't stop there, we headed on up to Park St and the Mauretania where Mum sang to the troops in the evening. About 9pm that night just eight days after leaving, two disheveled but proud faces had noses pressed to the porthole windows of the Mauretania while our Mum sang in an amber glow to the armed forces.

The W.V.S. woman

CHAPTER 10.

It seemed to rain for weeks after we came home from Cheddar, and although Mum was cross with us for turning up again and making trouble for her with the authorities we were happy to be together again. It was on this occasion that Mum decided to change our names to WATERS because she had married Charlie and she wanted to avoid confusion I suppose. There was never any official paperwork done for this change. Several times we were visited by the W.V.S. and we had the suspicion that it wouldn't be long before we were sent off again from the persistent bombing of Bristol. Our Anderson shelter was waterlogged by now so whenever the sirens went at night John and I along with Mum and Aunty May would crouch in the cupboard under the stairs holding on to the gold cross that mum wore around her neck, until the All Clear went. My Gran slept on upstairs merely grunting as Aunty May left the bed.I remember the simple prayers that John and I squeezed through tears, holding on to Mum's necklace."Please God, don't let the planes come over tonight! But if they do, don't let them drop bombs on Bristol, but if they do, don't let them hit our place.., but if they do, don't let us be killed" It was a prayer you could start when the sirens went, and add to as the course of the war changed overhead. It's uncanny to realize what skills were developed in the face of abject terror at the time. It's a fact that all the kids I knew then were able to tell what sort of aircraft was approaching by the sound of its engines. The siren would wail in that urgent undulating tone that turned your bowels to water, and as all the lights went out and the searchlights came on, a tense stillness would come over everything. You strained to pick up the first drone of engines. "It's all right, they're ours" someone would say, and we'd breathe again. But, if the continuous sound of the All Clear didn't sound, you knew you could expect more.

Often a small group or even a single aircraft would pass over in the black night and it was easier to isolate whether we were under threat from Dorniers, Fockewulfs, Junkers 88s or Messerschmidt fighters. This specialized knowledge was reinforced by posters and charts that seemed to be everywhere, which showed the black silhouette of enemy aircraft from the side and underneath view. I was a bit surprised when I later saw at close quarters a Fockewulf that had been shot down on Durdham Downs. A sleek brown machine that wasn't black at all. Nights of particularly heavy raids would have the Bristol skies throbbing as squadron after squadron of German bombers made their way up the Avon and then the Severn Rivers, navigating by the moon's reflection on the water as all lights were out. They were usually on course for the industrial area of the Midlands. "Birmingham's gonna get it tonight" we'd be saying. At the same time we knew that they would be coming back the same way, always with a bit left over for us and the docks at Avonmouth. There'd be fears, tears and trepidation all through the night until they'd passed over again.

School was back in operation again now, but earlier in the war they had all closed because kids from 5 to 15 had been evacuated to the country or smaller towns. When so many came back as we did there were hundreds simply roaming the streets. Many parents were resolved that they wouldn't send their kids away again and they were threatened with prosecution. The sheer weight of numbers compelled the government to open schools again and they kept going as best they could with a floating roll. It's not too surprising that children had some definite opinions on the situation which varied according to their personal circumstances. Ten year olds would say "War's a damn nuisance, everything's rationed, you can't even get sweets" While, Thirteen year olds would believe that "There never ought to be wars, if we were governed properly, trouble is there's always old people in power and you grow up restless. I've been to so many schools since the wars been on I can't settle down".

Shopkeeper – "You can't 'ave them..you aint got nuff points"

Pursuit of an education was a crusade for some people while others picked up what they could when the conditions suited them. John and I fell into this latter category, though we weren't delinquent. Too damn tired to be naughty! Well, for the most part. When schools were closed it was the right climate for juvenile crime and I know of many at the time who were offside with the police for petty theft and looting. This resulted in large numbers being sent to Church Homes, Orphanages and Institutions such as the Reformatory at Kingswood. Because of their young age, it's reasonable to assume that many of these were evacuees who had not yet made it home.

I remember how proud Mum was of her nylon stockings, when she could get them. I think the American servicemen were the main source of this desirable commodity. Without them it was common practice to paint the legs with a tanning cosmetic, which, if unaffordable found a reasonable substitute in watered down Bisto. In order to complete the illusion, a seam had to be drawn in carefully down the back of the calf and ankle with an eyebrow pencil or sometimes a burnt matchstick. This was a precision job usually delegated to Aunty May, but if she wasn't available John or I did it for her. Not always successfully, I might add, but then I can't remember ever seeing a lady with perfectly straight seams on her stockings in those days. When her birthday was due that September, John and I decided to get Mum some nylons. The best source of supply, being the Yanks. Why this should be I don't know. You also seemed to have a better chance of trading with them if you had a sister to introduce to them. However, with the resourcefulness peculiar to kids with a mission and armed with the knowledge we had gained of G.I. requirements back on the road from Cheddar, we began an active campaign of collecting and swapping to get the very best quality comics that we could find. They had to be clean, not torn and of the type that typified adventure and/or mystery. Comics like the "Wizard" "Hotspur" or the "Champion". While accumulating the stock we spent some time quizzing the G.I.s who frequented Scapens Pub on the corner of Monk St. We would show samples of the comics and offer another dozen just as good in exchange for a pair of nylon stockings. As the 18th drew nearer our hopes diminished. We had long reached our target of 25 good comics without arousing much interest from our chosen market. I think we had all but given up on the idea and were entertaining the sale of the comics to buy some smelly soap when John made a breakthrough. It must have been about the 15th and John rushed in breathlessly from the street. He said he'd just come past Scapens and a Yank we'd talked to a few days before asked him if he still had the comics. He said he would bring the nylons the next evening and we had to meet him outside Scapens with the comics at 7pm. I've never known 24 hours go so slowly. The Yank was as good as his word, and better! The formal exchange took place at the appointed time next evening. When the morning of Mum's birthday arrived we all sat on the bed to enjoy her open mouthed delight at her present of four pairs of nylons. The yank must have been a fast reader though because he left the comics with Mr Scapen to return to us, and as a result we were able to swap them again as we worked towards Guy Fawkes Day which was coming up pretty soon.

CHAPTER 11.

The priority for evacuation in Britain's wartime fell into very simple categories. They were "A" top priority. Schoolchildren aged five to fifteen. "B" children under five. Categories "C" and "D" covered the blind and expectant mothers. For some time many children had been evacuated overseas but this was terminated by Mr Churchill when a ship known as the "City of Benares" was torpedoed just two days out of Liverpool with the loss of many evacuees. Sadly the administration of settling children away from their mothers in "so called" safe areas presented other problems than homesickness. Where there were not sufficient billets in a town or village, the billeting officer was empowered to place children with unwilling foster homes. Consequently there were cases of five year olds being fostered by people in their eighties who had never had children of their own, or in some cases fifteen year old girls were placed with forty year old farmers who were exempt from serving in the forces. If you had the room you could expect to have evacuees placed with you. Imagine too, the children sent to Wales and were placed in homes and schools where they only spoke Welsh. The social fabric of Britain became very frayed around the edges.

The authorities misguidedly thought that we were safer away from Bristol and umpteen miles away from home and mother. At the age of seven and eight, I had very few priorities, but home and Mum certainly came at the top of the list. Part of Jerry's conspiracy of course was to persuade England that the bombs dropped outside of Bristol were less lethal. I could tell them otherwise after being bombed out of three evacuation billets in the space of nine months. But having the roof blown off or being the only house in the street left standing, didn't begin to approach the dangers inherent in trying to get back home once the misery of separation took hold. We were aware too, that the number of points in your ration book tended to dictate your worth and your popularity as an evacuee. The one saving grace for me during this time was that I was always billeted with my brother John.

Following our successful escape from Weston Super Mare and Cheddar and being bombed out of Devizes, the faceless people behind the evacuation scheme decided on somewhere more distant and less appealing, harder for an eight year old to find on the map and certainly harder to escape from. About 87 miles away on the South Coast of Devon was Exeter. The train journey seemed to take forever and the countryside was distorted with tears. We arrived in the dark too which added to the difficulties because it was important to know where everything was when you were planning to leave again very soon.

On this occasion John and I were the only evacuees in the house and this was certainly better than Weston where there were five of us all in the same bed. The lady seemed all right and the food was good, so I began to think that this might turn out all right after all. John and I could take some time formulating a plan for the escape, instead of rushing in and making mistakes as we did on our first attempt in Weston. We had separate beds this time and that was something totally new to us. Certainly it introduced me to the experience of sleeping right through the night. Up until then we had always been put into the same bed and my brother had been an inveterate bedwetter since he contracted Scarlet Fever when he was five. We were given dressing gowns as presents and were given a small part of the garden in which to grow our own flowers. Did I mention that bedwetters among evacuees were worth 2/6d more per week? Amazing how that percentage shot up very quickly!! I didn't like the school there much, but on the whole this began to look like it might be bearable. The lady held your hand going down the street and took your cap off for you if you met someone. I felt quite posh!! Street activities were different from home because there weren't the bomb sites to play on, at least, not till Exeter was picked out by the Luftwaffe as a target following the bombing of Essen. It was harsh retaliation.

Back home these were our playgrounds for "War Games". Sides were picked by nominated team leaders (Never me, I was too small, nor Audrey, she was a girl). The leaders approached each other heel and toe and the last complete foot won first choice (never me or Audrey). The sides were always Rommel's men and Monty's 8th Army. Set out in some suitable open space we would join battle vigorously in what was called Desert Warfare. In simple terms this meant throwing handfuls of sand pinched from the sandbags to see who could be blinded enough to retreat. It was very effective and even those who played Rommel's men knew the wisdom of letting Monty win. Boxes or barrels were employed as tanks, and assaults with sticky mud bombs was the means of disabling them. Perhaps if these tactics had been known in North Africa, it might have shortened the war.

All in all Exeter was measuring up pretty well and the first four weeks went by without the need to try an escape back to Bristol. The Baedeker Raids were so named as this was a European map rather like the Michelin ones wherein the Germans selected the "Jewels in the Crown" of England as targets. Some cities were earmarked for retaliation and Exeter was to be one of those. The lady had a Morrison shelter in the living room that also served as the dining table. Caged all round and with a steel plate top it was rather like a large rat trap. On the night of the raid we were ushered from bed to the Morrison with blankets and everything seemed to follow the usual pattern. First the quiet following the siren, then the approaching drone of heavy bomber aircraft, the first crackle of anti-aircraft fire followed by the crump of the first bombs. You almost burst from your skin with the tension, and your teeth hurt as you gritted them so hard. Usually it was over in about fifteen minutes and as the sound of heavy engines faded away we uncurled and started to talk again. It's funny to think how we all seek safety by wrapping arms about the head. But then! The world erupted! I can't describe the volume of noise that filled the house, as a lone aircraft following the main bunch dropped his stick of high explosives.

How many houses in the street suffered direct hits and how

many were reduced to rubble by the blast, I don't know, but when daylight dawned there was only one house left standing in the entire street albeit without a roof on it. Jerry had made sure that this house would be a useless haven for two Bristol evacuees and, following a couple of nights bedded down at the school we were back on the train and going home. "Thanks Goering" It must have been just before Christmas 1943 that we chuffed our way back into Temple Meads Station, past all the hoarding signs which said all the familiar things like "AH BISTO" or "SUPPORT THE WAR EFFORT.BUY BONDS" and "IS YOUR JOURNEY REALLY NECESSARY?" As evacuees we felt we had the right answer for that one."YOUR COUNTRY NEEDS YOU" was everywhere, and the bold print poster that said "DON'T TALK" was contradicted by the one that said "TELL YOUR A.R.P. WARDEN,HE KNOWS WHAT TO DO"

The two nights bedded down in scruffy blankets at the school gave us two weeks more off in Bristol because we'd both caught the highly contagious skin disease of "Scabies" The terrible itch and the ever weeping sores were only soothed by regular visits to the clinic at the Royal Infirmary where we were bathed and smothered with a blue jelly like soap. It was at this time too that a mass inoculation programme was in place and you were allowed to wear a red armband to warn people not to hit you on your sore arm. It didn't work with most kids our age. It's not only bulls that respond to a red rag.

The snow was heavy that Christmas, and a fashionable mode of dress comprised two pairs of socks on your hands, a scarf covering your head and ears, knotted under your chin crossed over your chest and tied at the back. All this, over the top of your overcoat. If you could afford some hot chestnuts from the street seller you could warm your pockets with them for a while. Not much you could do about your feet, they were always wet it seemed.

Christmas was memorable for the Carol Singing and the knocking on doors. The warmth, and the love of people who cared. In those days everybody seemed to care a great deal more than they did when the war was over. I remember too the stocking which had an orange and two bright copper pennies alongside the main present. (A second hand roller skate for the left foot only). But what a treasure to share with the street gang. I don't think we were able to eat anything that was particularly Christmas fare that year, but I have happy memories of the foods that we enjoyed in those days. My mother would make bread pudding in a large meat tray. It was a moist heavy stodge sweetened with sultanas and with a crispy top that you cut into slices. This was nothing at all to do with "Bread and butter pudding" as some would insist. There were "Chitlings" and "Faggots" the former being pig intestine and the latter like a small haggis. So Christmas was filled with tasty food, occasional dry warmth and plenty of copies of the "Beano" and the "Dandy" each of which were sold with a licorice stick or a sherbert dab in the centre pages. There were copies too of the "Lion' the "Hotspur" "Chips Own" and the irresistible "Champion" Jerry seemed to have taken a holiday at this time and so too had the evacuation authorities. We dared not think of it or even discuss it, just in case it jogged someone's memory. Mind you it hadn't been too bad at the last place. When the dreaded moment came, it was quite sudden and unexpected and we had begun to feel that we were home for good. Mum had changed our name to Waters since she had married Charlie so I imagine that this confused the authorities somewhat. I was not at all confused having got used to being someone else at the billet in Weston.

It was the last week of January 1944 when Mum, dressed in her railway uniform and headscarf took us to the pictures at the Metropole for a special treat. When we got home she sat us down at the scullery table and said. "I'm sorry my loves, but they've found you another billet back down there in Exeter" It was barely four or five weeks after being bombed out of Exeter that we found ourselves back on the train heading there again. Ah Well! We got to spend Christmas back home in Bristol. Our destination this time was the home of a middle aged couple who had no children of their own. To avoid further confusion for the billeting authority our names went back to Beachem as Mum had never filed any papers to call us Waters. The couple lived at the edge of a heavily wooded area on the outskirts of the city, and I mention the woods because they played a large part in our lives at the time, and they disguised a balloon barrage base staffed by a few men and a substantial number of WAAFS. These balloons were enormous gas filled silver grey monsters that ascended several feet up and were tethered to the ground with thick wire cables. They had large ears too and looked very like floating elephants up there. The purpose of them was to prevent low flying aircraft from making successful bombing runs, and, of course from planes landing. No doubt they were the origin of the expression "The balloon's gone up" just prior to some action taking place.

The first few days at our new billet were fairly uneventful as John and I got to know Mr and Mrs Dawson, and they got to know us. The best memory I have of them is that they looked like brothers. Mrs Dawson had short hair, which was unusual for a woman in the 1940s Mr Dawson always wore a waistcoat over a collarless shirt and he displayed a number of pencils in his top pocket. Mrs Dawson also wore a waistcoat so, apart from some variation in their clothing, they were one and the same person to me.

Once the initial period was over, we were assigned our duties. Blacking the stove and cleaning boots was something that we brought considerable experience to, but scrubbing floors and whitewashing the scullery and outdoor lavatory was something new, and I might say, hoeing the garden wasn't half as pleasurable as it had been when we were allowed to grow our own flowers at the last billet. The daily household jobs were to be completed before going to school so early rising at 6am was enforced. After school and before bedtime there were other tasks along with hymn learning or bible reading. We would be rewarded with a tablespoon of Castor Oil because it was "GOOD FOR YOU!" All of this was compounded by the weekend collection of firewood which seemed to involve everyone in Exeter. The requirement to attend Sunday church morning, afternoon and evening along with being in the choir should have placed us in the front line for salvation during this time. But I doubt that it did for it took very little more than a furtive glance between John and I to confirm that an escape plan had to be embarked upon as soon as possible.

Now, I really did eat almost anything as a kid. Wartime was no time to be fussy over food, but I found that my stomach revolted over boiled potatoes for one and also the margarine that tasted like liquid rubber. It was hard to avoid the margarine as slices of bread were always pre spread. But with juvenile cunning, latent acting ability and sleight of hand, the boiled potatoes found their way into my trouser pockets. I escaped detection for some time, but ignorance of the starching quality of potatoes was to be my undoing.

One weekend when the washing was being done, I was questioned by Mrs Dawson on the stiffness of my trouser pockets. Honesty, I was assured would spare me any punishment so naturally I made a clean breast of it there and then. I told her of my inability to stomach boiled potatoes and how I spirited them from my plate to the lavatory by means of my pockets. Perhaps a moment's pause preceded the biggest hiding I can ever remember getting. From then on I was very judicious and sparing with my choices of truthfulness, just in case!! Many subsequent meals found me alone at a separate table with bread, margarine and cheese. I would suffer the bread and marg as I pushed the square of cheese to one corner of the slice, knowing that the final two mouthfuls with the cheese added would make the whole thing bearable and hold my stomach down. Excursions to the woods, with a handcart for firewood collection was a regular Saturday feature. This gave John and I the chance to meet up with Mary again. She was the WAAF from the balloon barrage base whose generous helpings of bacon and eggs through the cookhouse window, placed her among the immortals like Monty, Churchill, Gran and our Mum.

The final straw for me at this billet was when I caught the Mumps. Painful indeed and the swelling made you look like a mating bullfrog. What humiliation I suffered by being sent off to school wearing a "Pixiehood" hat. This was strictly girl wear and my embarrassment in the face of laughter and scorn simply destroyed me and I vowed to quit Exeter as soon as possible. John was now nearly eleven and was allowed to have a paper round.

Although he earned more, he was only allowed to keep sixpence. Mr and Mrs Dawson applied new rules that meant we were not allowed inside the house after school until 5pm when Mr Dawson came home from work and we were to eat separately in the scullery.

John and I were somewhat blessed with good soprano voices and shortly after arriving at the Dawson's we were taken on as members of the choir at" St.Marys by the Steps" We were spending most of every Sunday at services in the church with the Dawsons anyway. I've never met anybody since with a greater desire for an afterlife. Every Sunday two angelic junior members of the choir in red cassocks and white surplices took up the collection down the aisles of St Marys and smiled at each member of the congregation as they made their tribute. John and I had decided that the best way to get home was to take the normal route and method that anybody else would if they didn't want to arouse suspicion. We'd had the experience of running away in Weston Super Mare and not being well enough prepared to avoid questions and ultimate recapture. So, this time we planned a very casual trip back to Bristol by bus, There was a normal bus service that did long distance trips known as the "Green Line" It would cost us eight shillings each. With John's first sixpence we buried a cocoa tin under a hawthorn bush that Saturday when we went for the firewood. Every possible effort and endeavour was brought to the fore in our attempt to raise one pound. We needed sixteen shillings for the bus and we reckoned on four more shillings for food and special circumstances. The comics we had went very quickly at a Ha'penny each and John sold a rocket left over from Guy Fawkes day for threepence. We soon realized that our resources were few and the target a long way off. The bitter struggle with potatoes, margarine and castor oil went on relentlessly. We told Mary of our intentions and she gave us a whole florin which boosted our morale quite a bit. Yet, after about a month of effort we seemed to be at a watershed with our savings programme.

We were blessed with good boy soprano voices

John felt that giving his sixpence to the fund left him with absolutely nothing plus having to account to Mrs Dawson for every penny spent. Drastic actions were discussed, usually under the bedclothes at night and in whispered tones for fear of being overheard, perhaps not so much by Mr and Mrs Dawson, but by a higher authority. If we were caught putting this new plan into action, the shame and the disgrace would be considerable. But, I thought, "would it be any more humiliating than having to wear a pixiehood to school ?" How will God feel about it I wondered, but then, What about, "God loves little children" and what about, "God helps those that help themselves" Gran had often said that. It was all the justification we needed. During the course of the morning, afternoon and evening services on the following Sunday, with trembling but experienced sleight of hand, we spirited the balance of twelve shillings and sixpence from the collection plates all the while with heads seemingly bowed in reverence, though in fact, in mortal dread of being struck by lightning at any minute.

Supposedly off to school the next morning, we boarded the Greenline bus for Bristol unseen and we arrived home with four shillings to spare as we hadn't the stomach to spend it en route. Mum was not at all pleased at our arrival back but she was rather distressed anyway because she had just recently split from Charlie Waters. I do need to add as a footnote to this particular escape, that twelve years later I made a point of visiting Exeter again and I went to St Marys by the Steps. I had then the opportunity to say quietly "Thanks for the loan" and I made a contribution to the Church Restoration fund. I also went along to the Dawson's house but I couldn't bring myself to knock. I got back on the train.

CHAPTER 12

Having arrived back in Bristol unofficially from Exeter, it wasn't surprising to find that there weren't too many other kids around to play with and school at Newfoundland Road was only part time. There were stories in abundance of other runaways and one or two of kids sent to Barnardo's Orphanage because they returned to find their family had been killed in the Air Raids. Most of those at school were older than us, so we found ourselves with plenty of time on our hands which might have been dangerous given our adventurous spirit. I suspect that we were far from being ideal pupils even under the best conditions, but we did seem to score more than our share of what was known as "A Whack of the Dap" This was a punishment more painful for the humiliation than the pain inflicted. The "Dap" was the sole of a shoe known as "Plimsolls" but commonly called "Daps" in Bristol. At school it was kept in a glass case on the wall in the hall and its' ceremonial opening was always met with much cringing by everyone. The miscreant would be required to bend over in front of the class. Very few of us had much seat to the trousers anyway and I don't think underpants had been invented then, so I can't say it didn't hurt a bit. But being bent over in front of the class and whacked several times on the bum was hard to take without tears. Miss Fisk, our headmistress must have had a quota of whackings that she had to give in any one week and when the school roll was so depleted by absent evacuees, it meant there was more to be shared with just a few of us.

A favourite classroom game was a kind of medieval slingshot attack on the far row of kids. It meant pairing up because you had to use the braces of a partner to fire your ruler through the air. The ruler would be balanced on your partners shoulder and pinched back with the elastic braces. Then you would instruct up or down

Blitz Kids

and left or right to adjust your aim before releasing the lethal 12
inch missile. Given the time you could paint the end of the ruler
with ink from your inkwell. Dart attacks were popular too and
easily made by breaking the point off an old pen nib and exposing
two sharp spears at the sides. Flights made of paper and often
decorated with swastikas. These slid into a split at the back of the
nib. These flew more elegantly than a ruler and were certainly
not as painful. As luck would have it I was spotted by Miss Fisk
through the window of an adjoining corridor while I was engaged
in battle.

Following her "Spanish Inquisition" bit, I was instructed to
fetch the pole that unlatched the glass case holding the dreaded
"Dap" I made for the pole standing beside the door, and at
the very last second my legs took over control of my mind and
body. At the greatest speed I could muster I was gone from the
classroom, the school, the dreaded "Dap" and I had placed the
length of Newfoundland Road between myself and Miss Fisk.

The deed was done before I could think of the implications of it.
Every second away made it harder to go back so I just kept going
all the way home. Mum was at work, I knew that so I went round
to our Gran's place in Monk Street." What bist thee doin' ere" she
asked."I've been bad Gran and I don't wanna go back to school"I
said "Gawd bleed'n imey, what you been doin' now?" I told her
all about Miss Fisk giving me a "whack of the Dap" all the time
and our John had it plenty of times and it was all over some games
we played and we weren't the only ones doing it but we always
got caught. Before I could finish Gran was pushing the hatpin
through her black hat and pulling me out of the front door by the
ear. She clipped me down Newfoundland Road to the school and
into the classroom. She stopped Miss Fisk in full flight and asked
to see her out in the corridor. What took place between them I
shall never know but I was moved to the front where I could be
watched through narrowed eyes and I was last to leave class at the
end of the day for weeks. I did avoid the "Dap" on that occasion
and when I got the chance I said "Thanks Gran" She grunted
something about tykes being the death of her and then said "Don't

you go bringing no more trouble home, think I aint got enough to do? There's a war on and I told that Miss Fisk to deal with you kids there, not send you home. You'll get more than the "Dap" if you come home again". I don't really think she meant it!

CHAPTER 13

After the Exeter episodes, I rather think that the evacuation authorities quietly dropped the Beachem file behind a dusty desk in the hope that it wouldn't be found again before the war ended. Actual figures seem to vary (never a good sign) but it's probably safe to say that over 4,000,000 evacuees were shunted around England and overseas. Many of these had been settled quickly and gave no cause for concern throughout the war and many came through with warm happy memories of that time. In the case of my brother and I, we seemed to have created a small mountain of paperwork and travelled as many footsore miles as an average Infantry Unit. I know from the many that we met and have spoken to subsequently, that we were far from being among the exceptions.

We were really a part of an unconscious wave of rebellion against change to the family unit, and to our socio-economic birthright. Perhaps being bombed out and resettled were categories for which there was some provision in the evacuation scheme, but voluntarily absconding from your billet, pinching your own ration books and travelling miles overland to get home again may have been a small file to which my brother and I made a large contribution. I'm inclined to think that the reverse is nearer the truth. Our misdemeanours were very small in the greater scheme of things. Perhaps it was better to accept our determination and lose the file. It looked like being home for good. I recently came across a statement made by Richard Titmuss, a noted social historian, who wrote, "To be torn up from the roots of home life and to be sent away from the family circle, in most instances for the first time in a child's life, was a painful event. The whole of a child's life, its hopes and fears, its dependence for affection and social development, and all the deep emotional ties that bound it to its parent, were suddenly disrupted."

From the very first evacuation in September 1939 It ceased to be a problem of administrative planning. It became instead a multitude of problems in human relationships. The "class system" of England was in for one helluva shock when country houses were introduced to children from the slums of London. In the same way, some middle class children found themselves in poor villages in Wales where no one spoke any English. The often uttered maxim rang true "There's a war on, put up with it!"I do believe that we as kids were bearing up better than most adults to the privations of war. This was surely because kids were so inventive and willing to accept new conditions and of course, to change them if necessary. I think back on the war games that we played on the very sites of real tragedy and death. The cardboard tanks we built, the sticky bombs we made which put them out of action. The knowledge of the rule, that if the siren went when you were on your way to school, you could turn and go home immediately. If already past the school gates, you were to stay. It was this knowledge that governed the pace at which you walked to school. The object of a slow pace was to give Jerry every opportunity to launch a raid before you got there. Congestion at the gates was caused by the desperate hopes of those who wouldn't enter until the last minute, and all chance was gone of a wailing siren sending them careering back home again. Raids which occurred while you were at school, brought into action the often rehearsed procedure for getting to the nearest air raid shelter. Large numbers of children were moved very quickly through the streets by what was known as the "Wave Method". This involved columns of three or four assembling on the pavement to march in a given direction and when the road had to be crossed we were brought to a halt. A loud blast on a whistle and we turned to face the opposite pavement then a second blast cause a surge like one body across to the other side ready to march on. Groups of several hundred were moved very quickly in this way.

The public shelters in Bristol City centre were of dubious solidity, built of red brick and designed to look not unlike today's public toilets. Most of them seemed to serve both purposes. They had an entrance at each end and a central dividing wall. The drainage and ventilation gap in the bottom of this wall was just big enough to squeeze through if you felt inclined to play the "time honoured" game of Confuse the teacher when the counting was being done. Many of these shelters were severely damaged during bombing and on reflection it was probably because they looked like military installations from the air. I later learned that Arnos Vale cemetery was bombed for this very reason. This ancient cemetery has since been closed for burials but I mention it because it is the last resting place of my father buried there in 1937.

Crushing dozens of children into one of these shelters was an oft repeated exercise and it was during one of these events that John lost his glasses. John had been a wearer of glasses since about the age of four and as any dependent knows they can cause no end of trouble in requiring the care and attention that a child is not used to giving. His glasses were supplied by the Corporation, as we knew it, I suppose it was the Health Department. They were the typical wire frame type of the period. I had seen them worn with one arm only for a long time and I was familiar with the sight of them in bits of plaster repairs. I doubt that his vision benefitted much from the appearance of bi-focalism that the crack gave to the lens of his left eye. So, the humour had quite gone out of their appearance when a jostling elbow removed them from his nose and dispensed with the one remaining arm. My lasting memory of his glasses is that he then wore them for over another year with two loops of string over his ears to hold them on.

It was during the lengthy times of being confined to shelters that the songs were sung and the charades performed and the traditions of British Music Hall flourished yet again. While the adults found hidden talents with which they could ease the stress, the kids gave birth to parodies, chants and graffiti the like of which still stays with me. The often heard Colonel Bogey March was given the lyrics." Hitler has only got one ball, Goering has two but very small Himmler has something similar, but poor old Goebbels has no balls at all." Whether there was any truth in it, didn't matter.

It gave us all a laugh at the time. Then there was the evacuees anthem sung to the tune of "Old soldiers never die".. "I know a rotten place far far away called (whatever) Where we have bread and jam three times a day. Egg and bacon never see, never brings us in our tea. We are gradually fading away." We all joined in with "We're gonna hang out the washing on the Siegfried Line" and of course "Run Rabbit Run" which we've all heard as the theme tune to the popular TV series "Dads Army" It was desert warfare on the bomb sites and "Convoy" in the gutters. Later in the war we invented "Concentration Camp" although the true horror of these atrocities against humanity were not revealed until they were over run. For us as children these camps were only known as the prisons like "Stalag Luft 3" where our captured airmen and soldiers were imprisoned. The game involved a team on either side of a fence or railing, and the object of the game was to overthrow the German Guards in order to free the weak prisoners. This obviously involved a lot of fence scaling. One such location with ideal iron railings was St. Mary Redcliffe Church, and the small scar on the inside of my left knee is a reminder of being caught up in the spikes of those railings as we were chased out by the Vicar. I put a jumping Jack in his letterbox next Guy Fawkes day for that.

The cinemas were beginning to show encouraging news items following that well known opening theme, and the voice that said "This, is the Gaumont British News..The eyes and ears of the World." Cheers would go up in the cinema when the Germans were shown retreating towards Berlin, or with newsreel footage of an enemy ship going down. I remember the night we were at the Metropole when a news item showed the liberation of the Belsen Concentration Camp and how the entire audience erupted in laughter when the stricken boney frames of the prisoners appeared in what seemed to be "Pyjamas". This was followed by stunned disbelief and horror at the terrible indignities that had been inflicted and suffered elsewhere in the name of war.

By late 1944 the war seemed to be losing its impetus. There were certainly fewer raids now and the blackout precautions had been lifted. Mum didn't have to do war work at Temple Meads

Station any more and she took a job as a "Clippie" on the buses. The uniform was similar and so were the hours so she still sang in the "Mauretania" at night. About this time we were introduced to a new "Uncle". He was a G.I. named Gerald Jennings who worked as an artist in the Disney Studios. Corporal Jennings was short, slim and balding and he was anxious to take us all to America and he married my mother to prove that he meant it.I was never fully appraised of why he returned to his unit and left for the United States without us, but these sorts of dramatic changes had become customary in our young lives. As it turned out this was not the end of the story and I jump forward in time briefly to say that Gerald Jennings turned up again in our lives when we had moved to New Zealand. He renewed his relationship with us in 1946 and moved us to the township of HAWARDEN just out of Christchurch where John and I attended the District High School as John and Kenneth JENNINGS.. for one year prior to his final disappearance back to the States! Another change of identity !!!

CHAPTER 14

An ever present column of jade green joined his nose to his upper lip, and to this day I couldn't tell you his Christian name. To all of us at Newfoundland Road School he was affectionately known as "Snotty Fox". He lived with his mother and three sisters in a Council house near us in St Pauls. His father just vanished one day some years earlier. He just failed to come home from his job down on the docks and the police were never able to find him, he vanished without trace. Mrs Fox worked at night in a bakery and then slept most of the morning, which meant that the kids were on their own for all hours at night and only saw their mum about teatime. Snotty asked her once if I could come and stay the night and she readily agreed. I suppose she was glad to have someone to keep him company, because his sisters were all older and involved with their own friends and activities. Snotty was two years older than me and about six inches taller. We were all a bit scrawny then, but he was bonier than most of us. His mended trousers, limp socks and unraveling jersey hung on his frame in a rather divorced manner. Though he sniffed incessantly, he did have two redeeming features. He knew everything there was to know about the more secret aspects of the opposite sex, a knowledge attributable to having three sisters, and he could run faster than anybody we knew. It was an ungainly style of movement though, and his arms held high with elbows out made it difficult to run with him without risking injury.

As arranged I went home with him after school on this particular day and willingly joined in with the round of household tasks. We had to get coal in for the stove that night, and clear out the grate. We helped Mrs Fox get the fire going under the copper as she boiled up the washing.

It was difficult to run with Snotty Fox without risking injury

We then held on to the bulky wet sheets as she twisted the water out of them before winding them through the mangle. It took the strength of all three of us to push up the prop on the clothes line when it was full. Snotty pointed out which knickers belonged to which sister and we stifled giggles in our hands. Joan, Sarah and Pat were all busy preparing the tea indoors, and the two younger ones were in something of a rush to get off to their "Band of Hope" meeting at St Pauls church hall down the road. Tea was just bread, of which there was plenty, and jam of which, there was very little. Followed by cocoa without milk. Mrs Fox went off to her job at the bakery leaving Snotty and myself along with his eldest sister Joan to keep the fire in till the others came home again. "Let's go door knockin" said Snotty. "All right" I said. So we tied our scarves round our faces as masks and went out into the damp Bristol streets. This game was new to me and I didn't really know what was going on when Snotty went up to someone's door and loudly rapped the iron knocker. He then bolted up the street leaving me wondering whether I was supposed to know who answered the door. "Run, Run, ya daft bugger" he screeched. And I left the doorway as the owner appeared. He raged and shook his fist at us as we rounded the corner. My heart was pounding like a hammer and I thought my eyes would burst, when Snotty. just ahead of me, banged on another door before bolting with renewed speed around the next bend and leaving me in full view of the old lady who came out.

Snotty pointed out which knickers belonged to which sister

I was beginning to catch on. "You do the next'un Ken." he said. Two streets away from our first door I reached up at a Lion Head knocker somewhat breathless. Rising onto tiptoes, the door suddenly opened right in front of me. The doorway was suddenly filled by a belly and braces, topped by a red neck and face bursting out of a collarless shirt. I was thunderstruck and rooted to the spot. "Well, Wha's thee want then?" he roared. "Aah! 'ave you.. 'ave you um, got any odd jobs Mister, I'm collecting for the scouts" I said. "I'll give thee sixpence to get rid of all these old bottles." He said.

Within minutes I had recovered Snotty and my composure, had the bottles tied up in both our overcoats and we were on our way home with threepence each. From then on the game of door knocking took second place to "Odd Jobbing". It was easier on the nerves and better on the pocket. Snotty was evacuated up to Norfolk when John and I went to Exeter and we gradually drifted apart, but on the few occasions we met up we always had a laugh over that incident and I think we both learnt something from the experience. Later in life Snotty ran a successful business selling Army Surplus goods. The skill of turning an adverse situation to your own advantage is more common to children than to most adults. It certainly added to my store of worldliness that helped me get through childhood relatively unscathed.

CHAPTER 15

My mother, my Gran and also Aunty May would take turns in holding a place in a queue. These were usually for food or for clothing. Some were day long affairs and most often they were joined without any knowledge of what was being queued for until you got to the front. There were queues for bread or for meat, queues for the pictures. Places were guarded vigorously. The only ones to jump the queue were expectant mothers with a green ration book. Gran held no patience for pregnancy used in this way if it beat her to the best cuts of meat or the last few tins of pilchards. Those that were classed as "Eating for two" were usually encouraged to take a place at the front, with "Cmon love you get in here then" My Gran would grip her basket tightly and mutter." I'd give tuppence to find out if she had a pillow up ther" but she gave ground if she had to.

Milk was rationed to two pints a week and as a result some people took to keeping a goat and grazing it in their backyard. If you could afford the rent you could take a small allotment up on the Downs and grow your own vegetables.DIG FOR VICTORY was a sign seen everywhere. We couldn't afford an allotment but in very bad times John and I, Snotty and Dennis along with Audrey would visit the allotments to give them a quality check. We weren't very interested in the greens of course, but we were experienced tasters of carrots and tomatoes. There was the odd occasion when we would pick more tomatoes than we could eat, so we would offer the excess to other allotment owners for a reasonable price. Gran was always grudgingly grateful for anything she could add to the meagre rations and knew just when and, when not, to ask questions. Up at the allotments there was one shed larger than all the others. Most people had a small building about the size of a phone box in which to keep their gardening tools. This larger shed had a top storey of wire fronted cages. It was a pigeon loft. It was owned by a strange old lady with a long grey skirt and a black beret. She always seemed to be up there seated in an old wicker chair outside the loft, cleaning and grooming her pigeons which perched on her head or her shoulders. We decided that she was probably a loony, but curiosity being one of the failings of small boys and with scant regard for what Gran always said it did to "the cat," all five of us found ourselves up at the allotments one day when she didn't seem to be around. All was locked but there was a small window at one side. Climbing on Snotty's shoulder and clearing the grimy glass I could make out shelves that seemed to be laden with a great variety of tinned goods. There was Spam, tinned beans, tinned fish, bottles of vinegar or oil, it seemed like an Alladin's cave of special foodstuffs. We each took a look and then conferred. We had heard of the "Black Market" and felt convinced that we had found a source of devious dealings.

Gran and Aunty May listened to our account of the Pigeon lady at bedtime, then in the morning told us to say nothing to anyone about her and to stay away from the allotments. We were a bit surprised at this lack of action and we did stay away from the allotments for a short while but when we found ourselves up there next we watched the Pigeon lady from a short distance. She would open the wire frames and pigeons would take off in a flurry of feathers and grain. She would watch the skies as they circled the loft and finally returned. On this day as the pigeons were returned to their cages we saw two that arrived later than the others which seemed to flap about exhausted. She caringly dealt with each in turn and took them inside the hut. Shortly after this we saw a black car arrive to take away several baskets which were placed on the back seat. We were sure then that she was buying and selling black market goods to those who could afford them.

At this stage we thought it best to go to a higher authority than Gran and Aunty May, as it was probably more than they could handle. Without delay we set off from the allotments and called in at Ashley Down Police Station, there we gave an account of all that we'd seen over the last few weeks. The officer gave us a good hearing before calling in another man and we had to repeat it all over again. They gave us a cup of tea and a big piece of cake before putting us all in a police car and driving us back to Monk Street. Once inside and in front of Gran, the officer explained about the poster which said "Careless Talk Costs Lives" He said we had done the right thing by going to the police with what we had seen, but that the Pigeon lady was well known to them and she was doing important work for the War Effort. We were to forget about it and not go up there bothering her. This was reinforced by a clip over the ear from Gran when they had gone. "Why ever can't you mind yer own business when you'm told. Gawd bleed'n 'Imey Hitler don't need an army with you two tykes over 'ere".

"I'd give tuppence to find out if she 'ad a pillow up ther"

CHAPTER 16

The men who were too old for military service were asked to volunteer for the "Local Defence Volunteers" as the government hoped to build a home defence made up of a million of these men to represent a backstop should a landing invasion occur. They were known as the L.D.V.s but to the ever joking children this became known as the "Look, Duck and Vanish" They could be seen in parade ground drills using sticks instead of rifles and learning the art of tank warfare with home made Molotov Cocktails in lemonade bottles. They wore denim overalls and a tin hat. In due course Mr Churchill gave them dignity and status when they were issued with rifles and battledress uniforms and renamed as the "Home Guard" Mr Pym who ran a newspaper and sweet shop in Pennywell Road was in charge of a group of these L.D.V.s and they regularly paraded in the grounds of Newfoundland Road School. He was very proud to be doing his bit for the war effort and drilled his men fiercely up and down the playground. The local kids strutted along behind when they marched and scattered when they about faced. Now and then a sore bum was earned by a swipe from a broomstick that took the place of a rifle. They were though, an intrepid band of old guys who spent many nights on guard or fire watching duties, plane spotting and defence training of all kinds in order to combat a possible German invasion of England. Raids from the air very often produced a Dud bomb which would bury itself several yards deep on impact, leaving maybe a tail fin just in view at the centre of a large crater. This would quickly be roped off and the surrounding area evacuated as soon as possible.

The unexploded bomb or the UXB as they were known would be guarded until the Bomb Disposal Squad arrived to defuse and remove it.

The Local Defence Volunteers

Such a bomb hit the ground quite near to Mr Pym's shop during one raid and when it was discovered he was placed in charge of the guard who kept civilians at a safe distance. Mr Pym still had a shop to run of course. and he presented a comical figure in his boiler suit, tin hat and shopkeeper's apron while he alternately peered into the crater, snapped his men to attention and rushed into the shop to deal with a customer. My Gran certainly had no patience with him if he was playin' about with silly bombs when she wanted four ounces of fruit gums. After closing time he was able to devote his time exclusively to the bomb and its crater, and he quite proudly invited questions from passers by. The WVS brought the men an evening meal and once the guard duty schedule was drawn up, Mr Pym applied himself to assisting the Signalman from the Regular army in his efforts to contact the very busy UXB squad currently engaged elsewhere. After a couple of days of this the local interest faded somewhat, and there were other raids and emergencies in the meantime. Mr Pym, however, was vigilant as the barrier surrounding the crater became more elaborate. Signs and notices began to appear that made you think it might be an extension of the shop. Large arrows pointed to where he might be found in the event of an emergency. One sign explained that the bomb was known to be a 500 pounder high explosive and still dangerous. Mr Pym and other members of the LDV would sit around an oil stove and brew tea into the night, taking strict turns to march the perimeter of the large roped off barricade

My Gran took in washing and ironing as a means of earning money, and when she had completed the task she would deliver the basket of pressed clothes back to the owner, no matter what the hour. She harboured a contempt for officialdom that was only surpassed by her contempt for Hitler and all "the bleed'n nuisance the war was causing" Mr Pym barricading off Pennywell Road meant that she would have to walk a considerable distance further to get around the obstacle and complete her delivery. "Not with my feet!" she vowed, and ducking under the ropes she breasted her basket of ironing down Pennywell Road, and past the unexploded bomb crater. No amount of yelling "HALT" "Come back here, you could get blown up you stupid woman" could deter her as she roared back at Mr Pym in like manner. She continued on her way as she exchanged rude expletives with other members of the guard. My Aunty May gave her a right telling off when she came home and related what she had done. Gran was not only surprised at this but she was unrepentant. "If Arthur Pym wantsa put up bitsa rope every bleed'n where. He can do the soddin' ironin'. An' I aint buyin'my fruit gums there no more neither". Aunty May made some remark about the damage that this might do to the economy!

In the meantime the impact of the 500 pounder had broken both water and gas mains which resulted in a sulphurous vapour rising from the crater, and of course the loss of water and gas supply to a large area. The water seepage gradually filled the pit, and by the time the bomb disposal unit arrived there was a need for the crater to be pumped out before setting about the job of removal. New barriers were put in place and after many hours the squad were still unable to defuse it. They left for the night when the light faded. We never found out whether the bomb had a time fuse attached or not, but for reasons unknown to us all, it exploded that night, taking out a large part of Pennywell Road, six houses, Mr Pym's shop and broke windows for almost a quarter of a mile around. Mr Pym had gone off to help return the pumps and thanks to his vigilance with barricades and evacuation of the surrounding area, not one person was injured. When Aunty May read out the details from the paper, my Gran never looked up from her ironing.

Gran with a basket of ironing

CHAPTER 17

My Gran always found that her tea was too hot to drink from the cup, and having put in the milk and two spoonfuls of jam (we had no sugar) she would pour the tea into the saucer. Then with finely balanced spread of the fingers she would hold the saucer and drink her tea from it. It was a habit that the entire family indulged in and was typical of a working class household at the time. We would all sit around the scrubbed kitchen table at teatime eating bread and jam or a tin of pilchards while drinking the tea from our saucers.

Sometimes we had an OXO cube in hot water instead of tea or as a special treat "Cocoa". Towards the end of the war a new drink made its appearance at our table. CAMP Coffee. This was a thick coffee liquid in what looked like a Worcester Sauce bottle. A teaspoonful mixed vigorously in a cup of hot water with powdered milk called "Cow and Gate" was very palatable. My Gran. Along with two working daughters did their best to provide but there were many occasions when the money alone would not buy the food you needed because without the required number of ration coupons you couldn't make the purchase.

Meat was especially scarce, and things like a "Sunday Roast" were a matter of fiction. There were certainly sausages, and occasionally chops but never such things as steak. We sometimes ate rabbit, for special occasions, though you could never get that song out of your mind when you were eating them. Liver, kidneys and sheeps hearts sometimes appeared on the table, and Gran was a wizard with Chitlings or faggots and peas. Other cheap meals came from the fish and chip shop in City Road. Variety in those days was not a problem but the quality was always questionable. Therefore it was no surprise to see a large pot boiling on the stove one cold September evening. It was already dark as we came in from school.

Mum and Aunty May arrived home from work about 7pm. "What's for tea then Gran?" John ventured "Never mind, thee just better eat it an' be grateful" she snapped. John and I went out the back to play in the Anderson Shelter on the pretext of tidying it up. And of course, to pull one or two life sustaining carrots from the garden on top of it. It was a long time before tea. We hoisted Dennis in over the wall in a prearranged plan, because as two brothers we couldn't play satisfactorily on our own. We then set up house in the shelter by lighting the emergency candles with the (never to be used) matches, then sat around discussing the days events. Through crunchy carrots we roundly condemned Beryl Bates because we were sure she had nits. She was always scratching her head and when you teased her about it she came and shook her hair all over you..the dirty monkey! Audrey was always showing her knickers in the playground by doing handstands and Miss Fisk told her off good and proper. Did Miss Fisk wear a wig?? There was a strong rumour around Newfoundland Road School that she did. When Gran summoned us for tea with a "C'mon you two tykes" we blew out the stubs of candle and hoisted Dennis back over the fence.

When we bounded back into the kitchen it was to find Mum and Aunty May already at the table. Gran lifted the steaming pot off the stove hob, and centring it on the table she began to ladle the green mixture into bowls. "Wha's that then Mother?" enquired Aunty May as she craned forward. "Never thee mind!" said Gran. We all sniffed at the steam and probed at the jelly like meat that floated in our bowls. Without further question (for we all knew better) we set to, and Mum launched into an account of her day at work. The rest of the evening passed without incident. It was about a month later that this strange mixture appeared on the stove again. John and I arrived home straight from school one day to find Gran busying herself in the garden. We were anxious to make ourselves useful for fear of being sent away again. "Go on then" she said "Get theeself a jar an' help me get these off" She was removing the snails from a patch of lilies that grew beyond the clothesline. Within ten minutes we had filled three large jars.

"Give 'em yer" she said, and she took them into the greenhouse where she filled the jars with vinegar. This made the snails fizz like sherbert all over the place, and it also made them leave their shells. She then washed them in cold water and tipped them into the boiling pot on the stove. At some time or other the information must have filtered down from the upper classes that a great food delicacy was enjoyed on the Continent in the form of snails, and although we as children didn't question it, our Aunty May that night voiced her opinion. Gran looked very hard at her across the table, daring her to say more. Then she proceeded to ladle the mixture into bowls saying "If its good enough for them Frenchies, it's good enough for you my gurl."

CHAPTER 18

When you lived a "sheltered" life. And I use the term sheltered advisedly because we spent a helluva lot of time in one. The nights without air raids were enjoyed sitting around the stove listening to the radio. It was always uplifting to hear the tune of "Lilibolero" that preceded the programme called "Into Battle" It was a weekly programme that would tell the story of one man's war. I remember the story of a pilot who was shot out of his plane and with his parachute burning he came down in a small village in France. Eight German soldiers tried to capture him but he managed to kill them all. He was spirited back to England by the French Underground. I suppose that less than half the stories you were told were true as the propaganda machine was in operation to keep the spirits up, and it generally worked.

Although, when you had a raid such as we did wherein the whole city was on fire and the people demoralized, to hear on the news that the damage was minor and a great number of enemy aircraft were shot down, you knew that it wasn't true. Repeated doses of this misinformation lost Churchill much of his popularity and he was roundly booed when he made a visit to Bristol. Not wishing to give comfort to the enemy caused massive censorship on news and photographs. You could not print photos of sad looking people or evacuees in tears, nor could you show disrupted services or severely blitzed buildings. The bombing of the cemetery however was widely publicized to show the foolishness of the Luftwaffe. But there were, in fact, many mistakes made at times, some of which were only revealed in hushed tones, or not spoken of until after the war ended. There was the parachutist who bailed out of his stricken plane and landed in farmland up in the north of England. His broken English gave him no credibility with the local farmers, who proceeded to beat him to death with picks and staves. He turned out to be a Polish Airman flying with the RAF. Then there was the Canadian force shot to pieces with live rounds that were supposed to be blanks during a beach landing exercise on the South Coast. Fifty one died in that mistake. There were the evacuees and escorts who were en route to safety in the United States aboard the ship "City of Benares" She carried some 300 people. They were torpedoed two days out of Liverpool in the mid Atlantic with the loss of 260 lives, 84 of these were children. The "City of Benares" had on board Colonel J Baldwin Webb who was heading for the United States to urge the American government to enter the war on the side of the British. He was in the company of the German refugee Rudolph Olden. Just the presence of these two men aboard the "City of Benares" made her anything but a mercy ship. Further to that, the Germans argued that the ship was assigned to bring back a large cargo of war supplies from the U.S and Canada. At home in places like Bristol, Liverpool and Southampton, there would be a major exodus from the city between the hours of 6 and 8pm heading for the country and away from target areas like the Docks, then returning in time to go back to work in the morning. This attempt to avoid being bombed in your home often resulted in your home being stripped overnight by looters. Human nature didn't change because there was a war on. There was a very large scale operation in London that used field telephone communications to coordinate trucks that loaded up looted goods while the owners were sheltering down in the Tube Stations. Shops, factories and private homes all suffered losses on the home front which were not always instigated by the Germans "Makes you wonder who the bleed'n enemy is" my Gran would say. The C.O.R.B. or Childrens Overseas Reception Board was set up to bring English evacuees to other English speaking countries around the world for safety. Sending them to places as far afield as South Africa, Rhodesia, Australia and New Zealand. There are many interesting details contained in the C.O.R.B. files which have only been made available for research since 1980 at the Mass Observation Unit in Sussex. For example the Dominions let it be known that they wanted a balanced migration, a cross section of British life that represented both the rich and the poor classes. There was a request for "Only Pure Stock" which came from the United States "Interesting". Following the sinking of the "City of Benares" Churchill put a stop to overseas evacuation and brought about a law that prevented civilians aged between 16 and 60 from leaving the country. Having said that, do bear in mind that Category A for evacuees were those aged 5 to 15 This was a part of his policy of not giving comfort to the enemy who might have seen the exodus as weakness."Dunkirk" which we have heard so much about speeded up the need and in September 1940 the "SS Ruahine" steamed for New Zealand with a precious cargo of children, mostly from Scotland. The "Rangitata" and the "Rangitane" were other ships to be involved in this programme eventually. As it happened the "Rangitane" was sunk by German Raiders patrolling the South pacific. She was two days out of Auckland on her return with Child escorts and on Wednesday the 27th November 1940.the German Raiders "Komet" and the "Orion" who were flying Japanese flags. Opened fire on her that day at 3am..Six of the escorts were killed immediately and the survivors were off loaded on the island of Emirau where they spent many months before being found by the NZ Naval vessel the "Leander". These tragic affairs serve to illustrate that major errors of judgement proliferated throughout the war years with sometimes disastrous consequences. For those that affected children, the trauma continues on into their adult lives. Evacuees are noted for their emotional reserve which is born of their unwillingness to trust.

Chapter 19

Suddenly, Dennis Jay and Snotty Fox appeared back in Bristol, and though we hadn't seen them for several months, we picked up again as a gang right where we'd left off.

I'm sure that it can now be told, because the shop we all knew as "The Don" in Newfoundland Road has long been demolished and so has Monk Street. I always knew that some day we would have to confess. It was Dennis Jay and me that perpetrated the crime of robbery on this "Aladdins Cave" of Comics, sherbets, chocolate and small change. Dennis, like me, was small, grubby, impoverished and always ready to accept a dare, and this one came about by chance as we were playing on the coal heap in Scapens backyard. I had been lamenting the fact that we had no ration books having left them in haste when we escaped from our billet in Exeter and no ration book meant "no sweets " Dennis suggested that a ration book might not be necessary as we climbed to the top of the coal heap and he pointed out that we overlooked the back of the shop known as "The Don" As the coal heap mounted the wall almost to the top it was only a short drop to the ground on the other side where we were just yards from the backdoor. We found that the louvred window beside this door opened easily and within a matter of seconds we were inside a small store room. Beyond a curtained doorway the shop itself was bathed in a greenish glow from the street gas lamp that shone through the front window. Dennis, being a tactician and not of an impetuous nature whispered. "Tell you what" he said "I'll go out the front door and keep watch, and you can shove the stuff out through the letterbox" his gappy teeth showed clearly in the strange light and he set his lips firmly.

"Hey Ken, member that time we robbed "The Don""

Pausing only briefly to fill his mouth with wine gums from an open box on the counter, he undid the main door bolt and slid out of view. I looked around in the green enhancement of the early evening gloom. Then, stepping cautiously behind the counter I ran childish fingers along the rows of jars and the toffee tins. Lifting selected ones down it soon became apparent that most of them were empty and only serving to fill the shelves so I turned my attention to the counter. Wine gums! Yeah! Into the pocket. Sherberts? No time for that and too messy.. I pulled open a drawer in the counter and was startled by a loud "DING". Dennis immediately appeared at the window and cupping his face in his hands he hissed "What you doin' in there? Lock the bleed'n door case anyone comes" I moved quickly to the door and secured the bolt then opened the letter slot. "Hey Dennis" I said, "there's money in the drawer here." "Well, poke it through here an' I'll catch it in me cap" he said. The drawer contained pennies, ha'pennies and farthings. I scooped as many as two hands would hold and began feeding them through the letterbox. Dennis was giggling and we both enjoyed a sense of elation at the continued sound of coins clinking into his cap. I went back for more. Dennis remarked that we could come back in the morning and spend it, which seemed like a good idea. Coins of the realm continued to mount in Dennis's cap for several minutes. But then, I noticed a change in the sound. Coins seemed to be hitting the pavement outside so I pulled up the letter slot and called "What's happened, is your cap full?" There was no reply "Dennis" I called, I peered out through the slot only to find that my vision was blocked by a vast expanse of blue serge, then the contorted face of Dennis came into view with his ear pinched between a copper's fingers. It was a moment of indescribable terror, not so much for fear of the policeman but the thought that he would tell Mum and my Gran.

We had to put the money back, of course, and then show him how we got in. He wrote everything down in his book. At the end of the ordeal we were very sorry boys indeed, and we went off home full of foreboding about the consequences of it all.

Now whether or not it was the policeman's intention, we shall never know, but nothing happened. Dennis and I would meet and whisper urgently about it and we avoided going into the Don in case our guilt showed. None the less, the protracted time over which we expected punishment that never happened, caused a change in our behaviour pattern which lasted much longer than any recrimination might have achieved. I came across Dennis when I returned to Bristol for a visit in 1956 and as he approached me on the street he said "Oh! 'ello Ken, I aint seen you in a while, you

'ad the Flu?" Ten years had elapsed. Dennis and Snotty had both
been evacuated up to Norfolk and by all accounts had a pretty
good time on farms up there. Certainly never heard an angry shot
or a bomb. Snotty's story was a familiar one. He had been with a
group of single evacuees, that is, without brothers or sisters and
they arrived at the village where they were to be billeted, here they
were ushered into the local hall. The WVS and the local villagers
set about trying to place each one and we remembered our own
experience in Cheddar as Snotty described how the clean, angel
faced ones were snapped up first before he was escorted away
last of all. Dennis was placed on a nearby farm and they went to
school together, though they never felt the need to run away and
head for home.

It was good to be all back together again. Even Audrey showed
up. We would roam the streets accosting the Yanks with "Got any
gum chum?" They had a free issue and usually obliged. Many of
the servicemen that we saw now were the wounded who had been
released from hospitals, perhaps limping on sticks or wheelchair
bound. One told us of having a plate in his head, but I couldn't
see how that could be, because, surely the shape of a plate would
show..It would be like wearing a tin helmet all the time. Some of
them shook and twitched and you couldn't get any conversation
from them at all. Mum said they were shell shocked and would
be all right in time. The drone of flights of heavy bombers and
the sight of dogfights between Spitfires and enemy aircraft over
Durdham Downs had been finished for some time. Air raid sirens
were hardly heard and the activities of the city began to reemerge.
Railway Station signs and street names were put back up. Sticking
plaster crossed on windows to prevent danger from flying glass
was removed and you could have lights on at night without
using blackout blinds. Most important of all to the kids was
that you were allowed out into the fields again. Barbed wire was
removed from the open spaces where it had been placed to prevent
landings, and once more we had access to the good "Scrumping"
places. Scrumping was the word given to the raiding of orchards
for apples, plums, pears or any other fruits. We were very quick

to return to our favourite scrumping place out at Horsham. The Corporation swimming baths were only mildly damaged in the blitz and soon reopened. Although John and I couldn't swim, we enjoyed being there and we would wet our swimming costumes in the pool to show Mum that we were trying.

Apple Scrumping

Activities on the bomb sites too gave us hours of adventure and perhaps it's timely to note that when I returned in 1956 many of these sites were still in evidence with the rubble bulldozed into a corner and signs that labeled them "Adventure Playground" At the time we were only mildly deterred from using them when we heard of the deaths of two kids who tried to unearth an unexploded bomb from the rubble. The U.X.B Squads were busy for many months on this menace. Dennis Jay's father had been in the R.A.F. and he took us all out to Filton Aerodrome, which was a huge air base not far out of Bristol City and we were able to see inside a Wellington Bomber. Little did we know that a year from then we would be living in a city of that name on the other side of the world.

CHAPTER 20

A big map of Europe in the window of "The Don" showed that the Germans were being driven rapidly back to Berlin, and each morning the locals would gather outside the shop to shake hands and jump up and down with glee as little British and American flags were moved forward, narrowing the gap on the Russians who held firmly on the other side of the German city. We all made Guy Fawkes type images of Hitler and Goering and started to collect rubbish for a big bonfire celebration, because it now seemed only a matter of time.

Mum John and I were in the fold out sofa bed at 79 Ashley Road It was about 8pm when the news came that Hitler was dead and Germany had surrendered. All the windows in the road shot up and people were shouting to each other and hanging their radios out of the window in case someone hadn't heard. You just had to get up and go out into the streets.

The three of us headed for the Centre where everyone in Bristol seemed to have congregated, you simply couldn't move in the crowd. We lost touch with Mum and we got up on the roof of an air raid shelter and we were not alone. We got ourselves to a Grand Circle position by running over their flat tops and jumping the narrow gaps between them. Uniforms of all kinds were dancing and kissing and carrying each other shoulder high. No one wore their own hat and there was a bottle in every spare hand. It was the 8th May 1945 V.E.Day. We burnt our bonfires and threw Hitler on when the heat was fiercest and we sang "Land of Hope and Glory" through tears brought on by the bonfire and the sheer relief of having survived. "About bleed'n time too" was my Gran's reaction to the news of V.E. Day. It seemed only a short time later that the Japanese surrendered too and we were greatly surprised to hear that they had given up when only TWO bombs had been dropped on them.

79 Ashley Road

I remember John and I having our first haircuts in a real barber shop as a special treat at the end of the war. Up till then it had always been a scissors cut around any hair that poked out from under a pudding basin on your head. Mum at this time had another reason for making us look our best too because she was anxious for us to meet her new husband. It seems she married Jack Blackburn during our last evacuation in Exeter and he'd been away at sea ever since so we knew nothing about him. He was in the New Zealand Navy and with this coming leave he was going to take us to Weymouth for a holiday. He was a big hairy man with a wide grin of sparkling white teeth. Later in life when John and I were old enough to analyze all of this we realized that Mum was a double bigamist in reality as she had never divorced Charlie Waters before marrying the G.I. Gerald Jennings and then the kiwi sailor Jack Blackburn. The Weymouth holiday never happened though because Jack was recalled hurriedly to his ship and she set sail for New Zealand for a thing called being

"Demobbed" That brief meeting with him was the only time I ever saw him. Jack was offloaded at Colombo in Ceylon and there he died of smallpox in late 1945 leaving my mother as an official war bride. So, once again a widow with this sad death, my mother made the decision which was to change all our lives. As we were eligible for assisted passage we were going to accept an invitation to live with Jack's mother Eileen at 33 The Terrace. Wellington in New Zealand. I remember having very mixed feelings about this at the time. After all, we had just finished what seemed to have been a 3 year exercise in "Find Your Way Home" and each time sent further and further away from Bristol to make it harder. Now we were all back together and the war was finished. Mind you, we thought it wouldn't be as bad as being evacuated because Mum would be going with us this time. But 12,000 miles did seem a bit much. I did a kind of silent pilgrimage around all the places I knew, saying to myself, "This is the last time I'll see this" or "This is the last time I'll do this" As it happened it wasn't, but as I gave my Gran and Aunty May a tearful hug and kiss, the thought was there and it proved to be right for Gran; as she was to die in 1951. Dennis Jay gave me a wallet as a goodbye present when we said our final tearful goodbye at Templemeads Station, and he informed us that Audrey had been sent away to a farm in Australia. We took the boat train to London and Tilbury Docks. The New Zealand Shipping Line vessel "RANGITIKI" was the biggest ship I had ever seen and she was black with two yellow funnels. Children were able to travel on the same passport as their parent and an investigation of the ships manifest for her sailing on January 3rd 1946 showed the boarding of Florence Elizabeth May BLACKBURN and two sons, John Francis BEACHEM and Kenneth BEACHEM. For most certainly our surnames had never changed from our Birth Certificate names. My mother paid very little heed to paperwork or legalities so perhaps it was not surprising that she changed our names to Blackburn on the voyage but there was never any paperwork to make it official. I discovered that her sister LILIAN known as my Aunty Lil spent some time at his majesties pleasure for Bigamy in earlier years and for my mother the name changes and disappearance overseas would have covered her tracks. We shared a cabin on the RANGITIKI with one other family which might have been a bit of a squeeze, but as it happened we spent most of our time up on deck. The entire shipload of passengers was made up of war brides and their children, some of whom were bound for Australia and others for New Zealand and following some early seasickness that everybody fell victim to, we settled into a happy and well fed voyage that lasted for six weeks.

The voyage wasn't entirely without incident, as we came via recently ravaged shipping lanes in the English Channel into the Atlantic and turning left at Gibraltar into the Mediterranean. We passed a mine or two gently bobbing in the waves a couple of hundred yards off our beam, and these were only the ones we actually saw. Bathing was optional, but we cheerfully lined up on deck in our swimming costumes for a hosing that knocked you off your feet, and there were free ice creams brought around on trays by stewards every day at 3 o'clock. To us it all seemed like one of those luxury Hollywood movies. I wouldn't have been a bit surprised if Bud Abbot and Lou Costello had been serving at the tables where there was even a Menu every day to choose from. There were lots of games and parties, organized dances and Fancy Dress events. There was deck tennis, quoits, horse racing and skittles. In fact a whole host of activities to keep you amused and healthy. We stopped briefly at Gibraltar and then at Malta before taking our turn to pass through the Suez Canal.

It was all so wonderful and exotic to see passing camel trains and the magnificent pyramids, in fact, just to be where so many exciting Champion Comic book stories had been spawned. At Port Said, the ship anchored offshore but was soon surrounded by swimming Egyptians asking for coins to be thrown down into the sea so that they could dive for them. It seemed a reasonable request to throw only the silver ones because the brown ones were hard to see in the murky water. To which effect I found myself holding only pennies and ha'pennies after throwing a shilling and several sixpences into the briney. There were boats too that came alongside that did a roaring trade in leather wallets and handbags. The goods were transported up to the ship's rail with an ingenious system of rope and basket on a running loop, whereby the basket would bring the goods up for inspection and the money for the purchase would be sent back down to the bobbing traders. It was here in Port Said that someone gave me a banana. I had never seen one before and had no idea how to eat it, until I was shown the method of peeling them. Passing through the Suez Canal we struck the bottom several times which was a bit concerning but the crew said that this was quite usual so we didn't worry, we passed through all the locks safely and emerged into the Red Sea which quite surprisingly wasn't red at all. We called in at Aden and then began the long cruise across to Ceylon at the foot of India. We basked on deck in the long sunshine hours and browned our very white bodies while sipping on long cool fruit drinks. Life was just wonderful.

Every now and then we threw ourselves into the compulsory lifeboat drills. We were assigned to boats and a specific discipline that required you to don a fore and aft life jacket and run to your boat station. We all became very competitive at this, which is perhaps not surprising. We had all come from a long term of drills and disciplines accompanied by shouts, whistle blasts and sirens. Was there any other way of life?. At least with this one you all arrived laughing. On arrival in Ceylon. Mum was allowed to go ashore under escort in order to visit Jack's grave and I recall that she was the only one to leave the ship the entire voyage of six weeks, prior to our arrival in Australia. A few days out from Ceylon some of the ship's crew were asking the question "Did you feel the bump in the night?" Nobody had of course, but this was the seaman's way of telling you that you had crossed the line of the equator. A great celebration was held on deck and King Neptune was hauled up over the side on a rope. He proceeded to lather and shave selected members of the passengers and crew with a gigantic bucket of foamy suds and a wooden cut throat razor. People were plastered with flower and glue and then hosed down with the big fire hoses. All who were on board received a certificate for crossing

the line and were declared "Pollywogs of the Sea" We next saw
land at Fremantle and there we said goodbye to a large group of
war brides and children about to make a new life in Australia.
Then after doing the same thing in Melbourne, the ship seemed
rather empty. A sudden change in the weather across the Tasman
Sea kept us all in cabins for the next four days but on the morning
of the fifth day it dawned beautifully fine and we were all up on
deck to slowly round the heads of Wellington Harbour. It was
7.30am on February 12th 1946 when I first saw the "dolls houses"
scattered about the hills of the capital city of New Zealand, and
each and every one had a red iron roof. One large building stood
out from the others as it looked like a monastery. We tied up at a
wharf called Aotea and by 1. 0 clock that day we were sitting down
to a salad lunch (or so I was told) because the only meals I knew
of were Breakfast, Dinner and Tea. We had been met on shore
by Jack's mother Eileen and we had walked from the ship to our
new home at 33 The Terrace. Mum had changed our surnames
during the voyage so that we would disembark as John and Ken
Blackburn and I suppose she felt the need to do this in order to
avoid explanations. As it happens it hasn't helped me much to
avoid explanations over the years and certainly the situation was
not greatly improved when around twelve months later the ex G.I.
Gerald Jennings turned up in Wellington and Mum John and I
moved to Hawarden just out of Christchurch to be known as
John and Ken Jennings now enrolled at Hawarden District High
School. This lasted for just one year before Mr Jennings decided
to vanish again back to the U.S.A. Reintroduced as we were back
to the name of Blackburn we have remained so ever since, but
obtaining a passport later in life was no easy task as my Birth
Certificate makes it clear that I am a BEACHEM. John and I spent
our College years at Wellington Technical in the Art department
which resulted in John becoming a very successful Commercial
artist, he married an Australian girl and moved to Sydney where
he has lived ever since. For my part, I returned to England a
decade later intent on becoming an actor. I was very fortunate
to have training under Sam Wanamaker at Liverpool Repertory

and then, perhaps foolishly, undertook to drive overland back to New Zealand, well as far as land made it possible. Therein lies the subject matter which is not really for this book because I need to reflect on matters pertaining to the "Evacuation". I suppose many evacuees felt the need to revisit their billets and I know that there were many who look back on extremely happy times. The blitz placed lives in great danger and this was a scheme designed to ensure that the younger generation would survive. However, the administration of such a precious task often fell into the hands of those who were unable to carry the burden of responsibility, and many who had been badly affected hoped that a return to the scene would repair some of the psychological damage. There are those too who never had the chance to return to their families, because there were fatalities that occurred through bombing in what were thought to be safe areas, and there were those who didn't survive because of neglect and ill treatment. My research in the early 1990's at the Mass Observation Unit at Sussex University showed that a significant number of evacuees who became lost in the system ended up in Orphanages, Church Homes and sometimes Reformatories. Many of these were then included in the scheme to be deported to other Dominions such as Canada, Rhodesia, Australia and New Zealand. I should say at this point that there was much that I was denied access to under the Secrecy Act and an embargo existed on much of the Evacuation material. It's well documented that Britain had a policy of exporting children through voluntary Church Societies from 1929 right up to 1967 and I quote from the "GUARDIAN" Nov.15th 2009.

"New evidence shows that there was serious unease in Whitehall over the policy of sending thousands of child migrants to Australia, Canada and other British Dominions from 1929 to 1967. More than 150.000 child migrants with an average age of eight or nine were shipped from Britain in this programme. It was only eight years ago that the Roman Catholic Church in Australia made a formal apology for abuse, including rape, whippings and slave labour, that British children had experienced at its homes and farms."

Most of these quite evidently came from impoverished backgrounds and because of the ages of most it's not unreasonable to suggest that a number of them were evacuees that were lost in the system. The promise of a better life was most certainly not fulfilled. It was only in September 2009 that Kevin Rudd apologized to the many child migrant survivors in Australia while in Britain Gordon Brown apologised to the British people in February 2010. We cannot change history but we should ensure that such a thing never happens again. For my part, the years have diminished much of the detail, though the pain of separation has always stayed with me. A confusion persists though as to what constitutes a rewarding childhood, because in spite of the dangers and privations, mine was one of great adventure and I am so thankful that John and I were among the lucky ones who survived it and were not labelled for deportation. Tears that I may not have shed as a truculent child found an embarrassingly full flow in the Archives Room at Exeter library during a visit in 1992. Among a very large pile of evacuation material I found a brown file card which they allowed me to photocopy. It named JOHN BEACHEM AGE 8 (Enuretic) 12/6d and KENNETH BEACHEM Age 7 (Rebellious) 10/-.

Householder: DAWSON, E., Mrs.					Sold: 24979
Address: 12 Kater Lane, EXETER					EXETER
Accommodation:	Residents:				Ward Reference
Name of Evacuee	Age	Date of Billeting	No. of Order	Weekly Amount	Transfers, etc.
Beachem, John (B)	8	1949 Apr. 28th.	BB. 3434	12/-	
Beachem, Kenneth	7			10/-	

Evacuation Card

Printed in Great Britain
by Amazon